**NAVIGATING
PRIVATE
COMPANY
GOVERNANCE**

Praise for *Navigating Private Company Governance*

"We see a material difference between companies with a strong board and no functioning board. Strong boards increase the value of a business and reduce the risk of ownership. *Navigating Private Company Governance* provides the roadmap to a strong board, in an easily readable format."
—**Mark L. Lehmann**, CEO, JMP Securities LLC

"It has been said that a good board in a family or private business has the highest correlation to their long-term success. This book is an excellent resource to installing an effective board for long-term success."
—**Henry Hutcheson**, President, Family Business USA

"*Navigating Private Company Governance* describes not just *how* to create good governance practices for private companies but also explains *why* private companies should make the investment of time and capital to establish these practices. Implementing these methods will assure the company delivers the results all the stakeholders are looking for. If you are starting your first board with independent directors or starting to refresh your board—start here."
—**Dennis Kessler**, founder and president of the Midwest Family Business Advisors and co-founder of the Private Directors Association

"Having served with Bruce Werner on a newly formed family-owned company board, I saw first-hand the value of applying his tenets for establishing a high-functioning private company board. *Navigating Private Company Governance* is a must-read for private company owners and executives seeking better outcomes for their company."
—**Liz Levy-Navarro**, Munich Re, Wilshire Mutual Funds, Eastside Distilling

"The author has real experience in each of the relevant roles: stockholder, CEO, director, and consultant. The result is a trove of actionable advice for private business owners who seek to improve their companies through better governance. The wisdom of his experience shines through, making this a valuable read not only for owners, but also directors, who can benefit from insight into the thought processes of owners."

—**Shepherd G. Pryor IV**, NACD Fellow, founding member of the Private Directors Association, and co-author of *The Private Equity Edge*

"In a field often dominated by abstract theories and conflicting advice, this book shines with its refreshing and practical approach. Bruce cuts through the complexity, offering readers a comprehensive yet accessible roadmap to navigate the intricate world of private company governance. From inception to optimization, every phase of establishing and maintaining a thriving board is meticulously explored. With this book as your guide, you're not just navigating governance—you're charting a course for a brighter, more prosperous future for your business."

—**William Tenenbaum**, Managing Partner, Lodestone Global

NAVIGATING PRIVATE COMPANY GOVERNANCE

The Savvy Business Owner's Guide
To Developing An Effective Board

BRUCE WERNER
STRATEGIC ADVISOR TO PRIVATE BUSINESSES

INDIE BOOKS INTERNATIONAL

NAVIGATING PRIVATE COMPANY GOVERNANCE

The Savvy Business Owner's Guide To Developing An Effective Board

© 2023 by Bruce Werner

All rights reserved.

Printed in the United States of America.

No part of this publication may be reproduced or distributed in any form or by any means, without the prior permission of the publisher. Requests for permission should be directed to permissions@indiebooksintl.com, or mailed to Permissions, Indie Books International 2511 Woodlands Way, Oceanside, CA 92054.

The views and opinions in this book are those of the author at the time of writing this book, and do not reflect the opinions of Indie Books International or its editors.

Neither the publisher nor the author is engaged in rendering legal or other professional services through this book. If expert assistance is required, the services of appropriate professionals should be sought. The publisher and the author shall have neither liability nor responsibility to any person or entity with respect to any loss or damage caused directly or indirectly by the information in this publication.

Much of the content of this book first appeared as bylined articles by Bruce Werner in Forbes.com and Financialpoise.com.

Certain diagrams in chapter 6 were contributed by Dennis Kessler of Midwest Family Business Advisors.

The section in chapter 7 titled, "Getting Started: Private Company Compensation Committees," originally appeared in an NACD blog. The material is copyrighted 2022 by NACD and all rights are reserved. It is reprinted in this book with NACD's permission.

The BadgerCo case study in chapter 9 was contributed by Tim McClure of Blue Oak Strategy.

ISBN 13: 978-1-957651-55-2
Library of Congress Control Number: 2023917873

Designed by Melissa Farr

INDIE BOOKS INTERNATIONAL®, INC.
2511 WOODLANDS WAY
OCEANSIDE, CA 92054
www.indiebooksintl.com

Contents

Preface ix
1 The Ownership Journey And Governance 1
2 What Is Private Company Governance
   And Why Does It Matter? 9
3 Defining The Goals Of Your Board 21
4 Recruiting And Retaining Directors And Advisors 37
5 Costs Of A Board And Compensation 53
6 Planning Effective Board Meetings 63
7 Role of Committees: Audit, Compensation,
   And Nominating 73
8 Board Function: Oversight 85
9 Board Function: Strategy Development And Execution 97
10 Board Function: Management Succession Planning 117
11 Board Function: Capital Structure 131
12 Board Function: Risk Management 141

Afterword 151

Appendix 163
A Chapter Takeaways 165
B Advice For Candidates 177
C Acknowledgments 193
D About the Author 195
E Works Referenced and Author's Notes 197
F Index 201

Preface

It's not about finding the right answers in life, it's about asking the right questions.

Having sat on boards for over thirty years, the right question to ask is "why?"—as in, "Why should I have a board?" Another important question to ask—"How does it help my business?"—is easier to answer. There are many books on how to organize and run a board.

My observation is that most private company owners don't think about what is outside their field of view, and that is where a strong board makes a difference. Owners with boards also tend not to think about how to get the most from their boards, and that is a lost opportunity.

Why have a board? The conversation usually starts when the owners realize that they and their team lack the experience and knowledge needed to address future challenges. They realize they need help, and project-oriented consultants don't seem to be the right answer. This usually starts when the business is in the $25 million to $30 million revenue range because that is when their needs exceed the span of control of the leadership team. There are numerous exceptions to this, but it all hinges on the experience and judgment of the leadership compared to their future challenges.

Strong board members should be able to ask questions that stop the conversation, cause everyone to pause and reconsider the issues, and then create a new and better outcome from where they were. They should be measured by their ability to add a new dimension that was not considered or thought possible previously. This is the benefit of bringing in outside experience and judgment.

Business owners should be thinking about how a board can create true value, and hedge against downside risk. I wrote this book so owners can have greater business success with less risk and less stress. My focus is on getting better outcomes.

Bruce Werner
Chicago, Illinois

1

The Ownership Journey And Governance

There is an old joke that people who start businesses will work eighty hours a week for themselves so they do not have to work forty hours a week for someone else.

In my experience, the people who own and manage private companies do not like being told what to do by someone else. The favorite motto of the private business owner is, "You are not the boss of me"—so the idea of private company governance might be an uncomfortable concept.

Sure, these owners understand why governance is needed by law for public companies like Apple, Exxon, and Google. As investors in public companies, most concur with this opinion from Investopedia:

> *Corporate governance essentially involves balancing the interests of a company's many stakeholders, such as shareholders, senior management executives, customers, suppliers, financiers, the government, and the community.*[1]

Since governance provides the framework for attaining a company's objectives, does it also make sense for private companies to use similar rules and processes to succeed?

What's The Preamble To Your Business Constitution?

Let's go back in time to civics class in high school when you studied something called the Preamble, which is the first fifty-two words of the U.S. Constitution.

No doubt your teacher explained that the Preamble contents can be summarized as a list of goals by which the United States would be governed.

Four main ideas are presented within these fifty-two words:

- Who is enacting the Constitution? "We the People of the United States"—the owners of this enterprise.
- Why is the Constitution being adopted? "In order to form a more perfect Union"—to have a successful enterprise.
- What exactly is being adopted? "This Constitution for the United States of America"—rules and principles according to which an organization is acknowledged to be governed.
- What goals are established by the Constitution? "Establish justice, insure domestic tranquility, provide for the common defense, promote the general welfare, and secure the blessings of liberty to ourselves and our posterity"—five ideals to strive for.

These are the rules of the road for the ownership journey of the United States. Let's put political opinions aside for one moment. There is great evidence that effective governance has been key to the success of the United States as a nation for almost 250 years.

Likewise, effective private company governance can be critical to personal and business success.

The Ownership Journey: Secrets For Personal And Business Success

One of the key issues to understand when you own and manage a business is the difference between working *on* the business versus working *in* the business.

While most of your time is spent working *in* the business, working on the business is where the high-impact decisions are made. Oddly, the time spent on these decisions is typically inverse to their importance.

To reinforce this point, consider the most important question: "Why are you in business?" Most owners don't stop to dissect the question into its parts. The questions are: What are your life goals? How does the business help you to achieve those goals: financial security, happiness, family harmony, enjoyment of time well spent? You can make more money, but you can't make more time.

Additionally, how does your business strategy enable you to achieve your life goals? The business is an asset, and it should be used to help you achieve your life goals.

From that perspective, it is easier to define a process to help you as the owner achieve your life and business goals. Where you and your business are today is Point A. Where you want to get to is Point B.

Once the two endpoints are defined, it is more straightforward to construct a road from A to B. Success is about perseverance and adapting to changes beyond your control on that highway.

Eight Steps For Your Highway To Success

Here are eight steps for a business owner to build a solid foundation for your highway to success:

Step one: Create an ownership strategy. Develop a statement of life goals and decide how the asset must perform so you can achieve your goals. These goals usually focus on financial security, happiness, ownership succession, management succession, and family issues.

Step two: Create a business strategy. Once you set performance metrics for the asset, you should flush out the business goals and strategies that will produce winning metrics. This is usually something like: I need to get the business to $X EBITDA (earnings before interest, taxes, depreciation, and amortization) and sell it to achieve financial security. So how do we get to $X?

Step three: Use capital and talent to drive the business strategy. All businesses need capital and talent to succeed. Private businesses are constrained in both areas. How much capital, and in what structure, do you need to fund the strategy? What talent is needed to execute the strategy?

Step four: Execute organic growth and mergers and acquisitions to fulfill the strategy. It usually all comes down to how to grow the business. How much future growth will be organic, and what is needed to make it happen? If organic growth is not enough, acquisitions need to be considered. If you need to make acquisitions, who are the targets, and how will you successfully acquire and integrate them?

Step five: Think about governance needs. While the focus needs to be on growing value, risk management cannot be ignored. What governance structures are needed to provide oversight and perspective along the way? How will outside perspective benefit the business strategy? What is the system of controls being used? If the intention is to own but not run the business in the future, who is protecting the shareholders? If you need to develop a board, how do you define its mandate, select directors, and run it to add value to the business?

Step six: Take advantage of conflict resolution and mediation. This aspect of running a business is too often overlooked until major problems arise— yet conflict is inevitable in business. It is how you handle it that counts. So what to do when people don't agree? The biggest issues occur within the ownership group, then within management. If your governance system does not have these mechanisms now, you will need to figure them out when conflicts arise. Perseverance and determination have always been requirements for success, although they alone are not sufficient. A good plan, adequate resources, and adaptability are required for success since the market is fluid and dynamic. A little luck never hurts either.

Step seven: Plan for management succession. Continuity of management is considered the biggest risk in business, but it can be managed successfully with effort. This requires looking ahead to anticipate the future needs of the business and securing the talent best suited to meet those needs.

Step eight: Manage the exit process successfully. Building a great business often seems like the hard part, but it is really the preamble. A successful exit of choice is the capstone of a great career. For many owners, it is also the starting point for the next stage of life. The goal is to have no regrets when you no longer own the business. So how do you get there? Understand that the decisions you make on the business are the ones that matter, and then drive the other decisions to make sure you get there. It can take time to develop this perspective. But if you talk to enough people who have sold their businesses, this theme comes out time and again.

With these eight steps in mind, let's consider the critical behaviors for success in a private company.

Critical Behaviors Of Successful Private Company Owners

There is a benefit to being in the right place at the right time, as well as being blessed with the skills, intelligence, and connections to achieve business success.

From my perspective, the robber barons, oil barons, and software moguls of the past were in the right place, at the right time, and had what was needed to take advantage of their once-in-a-century opportunities.

But that is not what happens to most private business owners. The rest of us need to play the cards we were dealt as best as possible. As they say, hope is not a plan. So what are the few critical behaviors that define successful owners of private companies? After analyzing dozens of case studies, I've found a few behaviors are consistently demonstrated by successful owners:

Maintain focus. Many entrepreneurs are known for having the high energy level that is important for reaching results. However, without focus, it is meaningless. You can run in circles quickly and still get nowhere. The simplest way to stay focused is to revisit your mission statement and key strategy documents when things get fuzzy. The reason to invest time in developing these thought pieces is so they become your compass when you wander off course.

Have tenacity. President Calvin Coolidge is credited with saying, "Nothing in this world can take the place of persistence." It is not enough to work hard; you have to work on the right issues at the right time. When you reach your limit and you can't work any harder, step back and assess how you work. Don't work harder, work smarter, and bring in help when hard work alone is not going to get the job done.

Practice adaptability. Charles Darwin's "survival of the fittest" is often misunderstood. From my perspective, what Darwin really meant was survival of the most adaptable. I believe the same is true of businesses that endure over decades. Great businesses can start to decline if they fail to adapt to changes in their markets. As owners age, start to enjoy their success, and get comfortable, they can begin to lose touch with how their market is changing. That can be the start of decline that is only seen in the rearview mirror of life. Practice adaptability to avoid this sort of decline.

Making adaptations is the result of seeing external changes and responding to them. Great business leaders build their organization to execute—while spending most of their time looking outside of it to view their world and assess the environment they are in. Get input from the external world, anticipate, and adjust your organization for what is coming. As hockey great Wayne Gretzky is oft quoted, "Skate to where to puck is going to be, not where it has been."

Set priorities. Business is not a democracy. Priorities matter because time, talent, and resources are scarce and need to be allocated to their highest and best use. That is what owners are responsible to inform their boards and management teams of. Owners, specifically, only have to make a few decisions: What business are you in? Who is running the business? What does the business need to do for you? Non-owner business leaders must understand that directive, translate it into a strategic plan, and execute it. Priorities are set by ownership and driven down through the organization.

Manage expectations. When you combine focus, adaptability, priorities, and a practical understanding of what your organization can do, it is time to manage your expectations. Be aggressive but not unrealistic. This is both for yourself, as the owner, and your management and staff. Two phrases that sum this up are stretch goals (goals that are set just beyond your known reach but not so far that they are unreasonable) and SMART goals (goals that are specific, measurable, achievable, relevant, and time-bound).

Ask for help. Don't be afraid to ask for help when you need it. This can be tough when you are firefighting, perhaps lack resources, or just having a tough go of it. Even the best athletes have coaches, as do many executives. Sometimes a few pointers are all you need for a course correction. Other times you need someone to tell you what none of your people will say. Whether it is a coach, a personal board of directors, an advisory board, or a fiduciary board, you should be thinking of your current and future needs and surround yourself with people who can keep your thinking fresh and your eyes clear as well as provide clarity of judgment for when you may become conflicted.

Hold yourself accountable. This is often the hardest task of all. Very few people do this well consistently, year in and year out for decades. Several of the boards I serve on were formed because the owners knew they needed outsiders to enforce accountability. This is a higher standard than, "Let's make some money and have some fun." This is the ownership version of the concept of continuous improvement.

There are many ways to grow a successful business, but the behaviors that create success don't vary much over time. How well are you demonstrating these behaviors?

Where Are We Headed?

What exactly is private company governance is the next topic to be examined. More importantly, why does it matter for private company success? These issues are considered in the next chapter.

Chapter 1 Takeaways

The Ownership Journey And Governance

Your ownership strategy should drive your business strategy. Develop a statement of life goals and decide how the business must perform so you can achieve them.

Manage capital and talent to drive the business strategy. All businesses need capital and talent to succeed. Private businesses tend to be constrained in both.

Think about your governance needs. While the focus needs to be on growing value, risk management cannot be ignored. What governance structures are needed to provide oversight and perspective along the way?

Plan for management succession. Continuity of management is considered the biggest risk in business. It must be managed successfully to ensure the continuity of the business.

Manage the exit process thoughtfully. Building a great business often seems like the hard part, but it is really the preamble. A successful exit of choice is the capstone of a great career.

Know how to maintain focus, demonstrate tenacity, and practice adaptability. Priorities matter because time, talent, and resources are scarce and need to be allocated to their highest and best use. When you see your situation change, assess the change, and adapt to the new reality quickly.

Manage expectations. When you combine focus, adaptability, and a practical understanding of what your organization can achieve, allow yourself to manage your own expectations.

Ask for help. Don't be afraid to ask for help when you need it. This can be tough when you are firefighting, whether due to a lack of resources or just having a tough go of it.

Hold yourself accountable. This is often the hardest task of all. Very few people do this well consistently, year in and year out for decades.

2

What Is Private Company Governance And Why Does It Matter?

In a word, it's about trust.

Salesforce CEO Marc Benioff is a billionaire who owns about 4 percent of the cloud computing software firm he co-founded in 1999. Before starting Salesforce, he spent thirteen years at database software giant Oracle with Larry Ellison. Today he's an angel investor in dozens of tech startups.

Consider Benioff's words about trust: "Trust has to be the highest value in your company, and if it's not, something bad is going to happen to you."

Private company governance is about building trust with the people who matter most: investors, creditors, employees, suppliers, and the communities you operate in.

"The nature of a private company means I look in the shareholders' eyes on a regular basis," says private company finance leader Don Solman. "In a public company, those shareholders are 'faceless' and nowhere near as engaged in the business."

Solman is vice president and CFO of James Richardson & Sons, Limited (JRSL), a privately owned and operated Canadian corporation based in Winnipeg.

Like Solman, many finance leaders in private companies agree that the best way to build trust is by keeping the business model working efficiently by implementing a suitable structure for private company governance.[2] Creating that suitable structure begins with understanding the corporate governance principles that inspire trust.

Understanding The Principles Of Corporate Governance

Every private company has its own set of ownership issues, competitive dynamics, and resource constraints to optimize. As you would expect, private companies vary widely on what they want their boards to accomplish. Setting these priorities starts with understanding the basics of governance.

Public boards typically focus on compliance, management selection, and compensation. In a private company, this need likely has a different slant. As companies grow, they benefit from outside advice on who runs the company and how they get paid. If you own 100 percent of the business, these issues are likely off the table.

That being understood, I've found there are three functions that are critical for private company boards to address: approving strategy and financial objectives; advising management; and being on top of oversight, risk management, controls, and compliance. Focusing on these functions can pay huge dividends, and they are a measure of the board's effectiveness. While agendas vary, each meeting should include elements of these functions.

Most private company boards are advisory, not fiduciary boards, and for a good reason. Owners want advice regarding these three functions but they don't want to give up control to outsiders.

To understand how the functions work together requires an understanding of how private boards operate.

How Private Boards Operate

These are the building blocks of a private board:

Board size. While public companies often have tens of directors, I've found private companies usually do best with five to seven people in the room.

Independence. A primary duty of a public board is to hold management accountable, so there needs to be clear independence. For private companies, good advice and accountability are needed from the board. The outside directors need enough independence to maintain clear judgment.

Committee work. Most private company boards do not have separate committees, although larger ones do. Managing audits and compensation requires experience beyond general management.

Leadership. Public companies may wrestle with whether the CEO should be chair or if the duties need to be split. Private companies typically don't have this problem, but they need to have a strong chair.

Board compensation. This is always a delicate subject, but it is not without ample data to consider.

Boards Should Prioritize Substance Over Form

To quote an ancient proverb: There is wisdom in a multitude of counselors. In modern lore they call it drawing on the collective wisdom of the team.

Board work is intended to provide wisdom to solve long-term issues, which is best done through active discussion. Boards should minimize listening to reports and non-productive group activities.

The best advice I received was to identify just a handful of critical questions for the board to consider while looking forward three to five years.

It is the responsibility of ownership to identify and prioritize these critical questions. It starts simply by asking, "What keeps you awake at night?" For family businesses, it may go deeper into the family dynamics that constrain high-priority business issues.

If owners are unable to distill these questions alone, facilitation may be beneficial. Sometimes talking to an unbiased outsider helps to challenge and validate thoughts and conclusions about organizational needs.

Roles & Responsibilities		
Group	**Frequency**	**Key Issues & Mandate**
Ownership	Annual	What business are we in? Who represents my interests? How is the business funded? What results do I expect?
Board	Quarterly	Elected by the owners Hire & fire management Approves budgets Major strategy decisions Oversight & accountability
Management	Daily	Report to the board Runs the business

Figure 1

Focus On The Specific Needs Of The Organization

I find the "1997 Statement on Corporate Governance" from the Business Roundtable to be highly applicable to private companies in that it informs owners on the basics of governance. The statement mentions that "Good corporate governance is not a 'one size fits all' proposition."[3]

I've seen this issue stump newer boards. No two boards are alike, nor should they be. Like a bespoke suit, a board is designed and made for only one business. When designing a board, each seat should serve a specific need: marketing, finance, HR, M&A, etc.

"Don't buy what you can rent" is the best mindset when selecting directors. For example, technology changes quickly but directors don't. You can change consultants as technology changes. It is better to use board seats for knowledge and judgment that will apply over a three- to five-year horizon.

Where do you want and need advice and counsel? When do you want it? How do you best take advice on difficult and sensitive matters? This leads to the question of fit.

A successful board is a matter of chemistry and fit. The airplane test still applies: If you would not want to fly across the country sitting next to these people, don't put them on your board.

But what happens when you need to change a board member? To quote an adage, "Change is inevitable, it's direction that counts." Let's turn our attention to making changes.

Key Benefits of Boards for Private Companies	
Perspective	Provide a different point of view
Experience	Share domain expertise
Relationships	Introduce important counterparties
Compensation	Assist with compensation plans
Succession Planning	Assure executive continuity
Oversight	Protect minority investors & stakeholders
Conflict Resolution	Private intervention

Figure 2

A Practical Approach To Revising Corporate Governance

Good governance has two aspects: legal and practical. The legal aspects are what is written on paper, codified by law, and enforced by precedents. This should be viewed as the minimum required but not nearly enough to qualify as "best practices."

The practical side is what determines how effective a governance system is:

- Are ownership's best interests put first?
- Do important decisions get made on a timely basis?
- Are decisions based on facts and analysis or whim and ego?

- Are conflicts resolved without making the situation worse?
- Are all stakeholders heard?

This has more to do with human behavior and judgment than legal constructs.

Public companies do not have many of the governance shortcomings of private companies since there is a legal framework and considerable regulatory oversight. Most of all, there is required transparency.

There are usually ample resources to keep the bylaws and policies of public companies in good order. The policies speak to conflicts of interests, codes of conduct, and whistleblower protections. The courts have made clear the consequences of failing to maintain adequate written policies and proactive oversight.

While outdated and/or insufficient policies are less of an issue for public companies, these shortcomings are more of the norm with private companies. For most private companies, if the bank covenants are amply covered, the taxes are paid, and the owners are happy, governance practices are not likely on their radar screen. That is one of the benefits of being private.

Most private companies, certainly under $500 million in revenue, depend on a few people for all the major decisions. If the business is healthy, there is no oversight—the owners can do what they want. Due to this, they often benefit from outsiders who provide these positive behaviors:

- A strong moral compass
- Clear examples of integrity and ethical behavior
- Demonstrated financial accountability
- Demanding transparency

The outsiders prevent the owners from living in their own echo chamber.

But when there is an external event or market shock, governance procedures are often found to be inadequate to address the needs of the moment. The most common examples are a change of control event, an unexpected death, or an equity infusion from an outside party.

This is why governance needs to be examined and updated periodically; it needs to be up to date before surprises hit. A thorough review every three to five years is the minimum owners should require.

Here is a typical example of why good governance is so important. Recently, I was elected as an outside director of a global service company. When the owner died unexpectedly, the equity passed to his wife, who didn't know much about business.

Prior to his death, there was no need for outside directors, and little in the way of governance policies and practices. The entrepreneurial way worked well, markets were strong, and life was good.

The bylaws had not been updated from when the deceased bought the business forty years earlier.

Since the deceased owned 100 percent of the equity, the bylaws were the bare minimum needed to acquire the business. For example, there was no nomination, election, or removal process for directors.

The spouse desired to sell the business, so her attorney suggested updating the bylaws as part of getting the business ready for sale. He did not want outdated bylaws or related matters to cause diligence concerns for the buyer.

The attorney suggested forming a board to assist the widow in managing the sale process. The practical aspects of governance had to be developed in real time. The best practices for governance include a diversified board with a broad range of expertise, defined roles and responsibilities for each board member, committees, clear accountability to a high standard of ethics and integrity, and performance appraisals for the board as a whole and individual directors.

None of this can be achieved by writing a document. It requires personal leadership for these desired outcomes to be realized. The attorney was skilled enough to know he needed to make sure the widow had the right board members.

Like many events in the business world, leadership needs to spend time, money, and energy on issues that may never arise. Leaders are expected to update bylaws, codes of conduct, and codes of ethics, and demonstrate and enforce desired behaviors. This is the essence of fiduciary duty. This is where the difference between an officer and a director becomes clearest.

Here is another example of what can happen when there is an unexpected death of the business founder.

Use Good Governance To Steer A Rudderless Ship

Even the most thoughtful business continuity planning will fail to anticipate every scenario. The unexpected death of a strong-willed founder is a frequent example.

Much like in the public equity markets, singular unexpected events can greatly increase or destroy the value of a private company.

Most private companies do not have well-developed succession plans, especially when the long-term owner and founder may be more focused on their lifestyle than the business.

A well-functioning board should be able to manage this scenario. When in doubt, the board is in charge. But what happens when there is no board? Who steers the ship? A recent experience highlights how good governance can help even in the most difficult situations.

Jack had built a good manufacturing business, growing it to $250 million in annual revenue by hard work and a bit of luck.

But the business revolved around Jack. He was too busy growing it to think about succession planning. So when he died unexpectedly, the business became a rudderless ship. The equity passed to a trust for the benefit of his family. The trustee was the owner's estate attorney, who had no practical business experience and was quickly overwhelmed.

A family confidant introduced me to the trustee. It was clear he was unable to define and prioritize the issues needed to execute his duties.

After a few discussions, I suggested this plan of action:

Review risk. The trustee had exposure as the sole director and as a trustee. He needed to review his legal and fiduciary responsibilities with his counsel and insurance carriers and assess his various liability insurance policies to make sure they were adequate for the risks he was bearing.

Establish protocol. The trustee needed to establish a protocol for interacting with the beneficiaries, so he could represent their interests.

Redo bylaws. The bylaws were written thirty-five years prior. They were antiquated and grossly insufficient for the current and future situations. The bylaws needed to be rewritten with governance best practices for what the business was today.

Revise D&O. The company's directors and officers (D&O) liability insurance and other policies would need to be revised to attract the outside directors needed.

Reassure creditors. The company needed to reassure its banks and major creditors that it would be stable during the transition period. Since there was no CEO, the trustee and remaining management would need to step in and make this happen.

Recruit outsiders. Outside directors were needed to bring the experience, judgment, and decisiveness the trustee lacked. We established a search process and found three excellent candidates. Since the trustee had no experience in search work, we managed the search, set compensation, and onboarded the new directors.

Once the directors were elected, we shifted into phase two, which was to make the board operational. The board needed a chair other than the trustee because the trustee did not want to be conflicted with his duty to the trust. The chairperson then created a process to manage the short-term crisis, in addition to developing an agenda for regular order for the board's business.

The next step was to establish the governance, compensation, and audit committees. The outside directors used their prior experience to get these committees up and running quickly.

Three items became clear:
- The trust wanted to sell the business but was not in a rush and would wait to get the best outcome.
- The company needed to hire a CEO fit for the situation.
- No one was in charge until the new CEO started, which was expected to be six to nine months away.

This forced the board to grapple with a new reality: It could not wait for a new CEO to address major staff and competitive issues, yet there were no worthy internal candidates to bridge the gap. Should they hire a consultant to step in and risk possible management defections? Or should one of the board members step in on an interim basis to provide the leadership that was sorely lacking?

This is what we did, and what I would advise you to do in a similar situation:

Work quickly. When the owner died, competitors spread rumors of financial problems to undermine the company's stellar reputation. Employees worried about the company's health and competitors were starting to lure key employees. Time can be against you after a sudden change in your business so get to work right away.

Analyze your options. Working with the remaining management team, we quickly conducted a SWOT analysis and assessed unit managers' capabilities. We identified several major growth opportunities that would be missed if we waited another year. The business had been undermanaged for many years, and this inquiry process revealed a strong, vital company culture that was looking to charge forward. When making major changes at such a pivotal time, look at all your options before determining next steps.

Adapt to the circumstances. My recommendation in this situation was for one of the directors who had particular experience to step in on an interim basis and guide the business before smoothly transitioning leadership to the new CEO. While ordinarily this would violate the board's oversight responsibilities, these were not ordinary times.

The board debated and defined the scope of the interim CEO role so there was no confusion on the transition process to the new CEO. Remember that good governance also means adapting to short-term needs.

When a sudden and potentially catastrophic event happens, work fast to mitigate the negative effects. Give the management team and employees the security they need to focus on their jobs. Do whatever you can to keep clients from being negatively impacted. Finally, position the company to get back into growth mode. As a result, everyone's interests can be well-served.

The Next Step

Effective governance for a private company begins with the board of directors. The next chapter will explore defining the goals of your board.

Chapter 2 Takeaways

What Is Private Company Governance And Why Does It Matter?

Seek wisdom. Board work should provide wisdom to solve long-term issues, which is best done through active discussion. Boards are responsible for oversight, strategy, capital structure, management succession, and risk management.

Determine board size. While public companies often have tens of directors, I've found private companies usually do best with five to seven people in the room.

Foster independence. For private companies, good advice and accountability are needed. The outside directors need enough independence to maintain clear judgment.

Assign committee work. Most private company boards do not have separate committees, although larger ones do. Managing audits and compensation requires experience beyond general management.

Name a strong chair. Public companies may wrestle with whether the CEO should be chair or if the duties should be split. Private companies typically don't have this quandary, but they need to have a strong chair.

Evaluate board compensation. This is always a delicate subject but it is not without ample data to use for input.

3

Defining The Goals Of Your Board

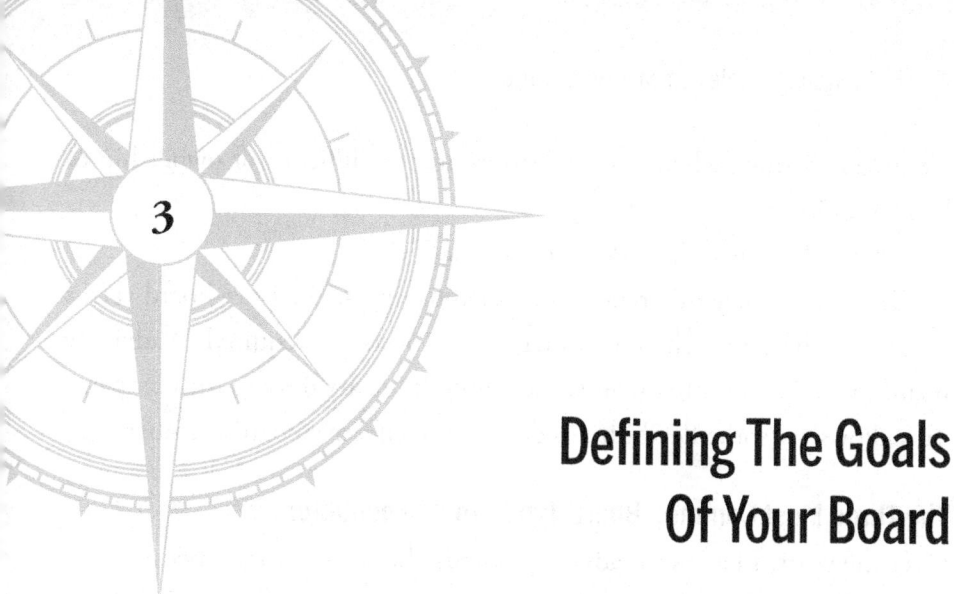

Startling statistic: From 2019 to 2021 there was a 52 percent increase globally in organizations utilizing advisory boards as part of their governance structure.[4]

My expectation is this accelerating trend will continue.

Here's why: as the business landscape becomes more complex and unpredictable, organizations are turning to advisory boards to fill knowledge gaps, provide market intelligence, and advance strategic objectives.

Boards of directors of for-profit and non-profit organizations have the same fiduciary responsibilities: duty of care, duty of loyalty, and duty of good faith.

While similar to fiduciary boards, advisory boards are not the same. The purpose and function of a board of advisors is usually not as broad as a fiduciary board, but outside advisors should conduct themselves with the same duties in mind.

What Does An Advisory Board Really Do?

Advisory boards are the manifestation of each company's needs. The breadth of subjects and depth of discussion vary based on those needs. Advisory boards are usually formed when critical matters are too difficult for ownership to handle on its own.

Ownership must then solicit outside advice.

There is one key difference when establishing an advisory board versus a board of directors. There is no regulatory oversight required of advisory board members. In other words, there is no fiduciary duty to the company. This allows for some flexibility in developing effective board members.

The Three Most Common Board Types You'll Encounter

Over the years, I have seen advisory boards cluster into three styles:

Consulting boards. These boards meet one or two days per year (e.g., when there is a pressing issue). The owners buy a day of consulting time from the outside advisors to focus on the issue of the day. Businesses with $20 million to $50 million in revenue may start with a consulting board before moving up to a fiduciary board. Businesses under $10 million typically do not have functioning boards.

Junior advisory boards. As businesses grow, junior advisory boards pay more attention to the following issues:

- Management depth
- Capital structure
- Long-term planning
- Competition
- Organizational capabilities
- Market structure
- Crisis management (usually involving the bank)

Advisors are raising important questions and helping to solve existential problems. However, the discussions often tiptoe around delicate issues like management performance, compensation, and succession planning.

Advisory boards. This type of board is most comparable to a fiduciary board. Outsiders are actively engaged in succession planning, management compensation, and management performance evaluation. This is more common with companies that bring in several hundred million dollars in revenue, because the complexity forces ownership to seek outside help.

At this size, ownership is keenly aware of succession issues. Since there is likely a mix of family and professional management, or a transition toward professional managers, succession planning and management training and development are time-consuming subjects for the board.

How To Choose The Right Board Style

How do you know which style is most appropriate? In addition to the needs of the business, the board becomes a reflection of the owners' needs and personalities.

Advisory boards are usually formed when critical matters are too difficult for ownership to handle on its own.

If the outside advisors are diligent before accepting, they will understand these constraints before the first meeting. Additionally, as the board's charter expands so does the drive to seek more professional advisors instead of golf buddies, lawyers, and bankers.

While most businesses strive to grow, their growth rate is typically not so fast that the demands on the board change quickly. (Venture-stage businesses are the obvious exception to this statement.) Absent a major change in the business, the type of advisory board is unlikely to change. This catalyst is likely to be a capital event, a change in key executives, or an external industry event that creates a shockwave or trauma that must urgently be addressed.

Sir Isaac Newton's first law of motion states that a body in motion stays in motion unless acted upon by another force. In the same way, owners tend to stay on the same path until the pain of conflict forces them to make a change. The greater the pain, the greater the need for outside advisors. Therefore, outside advisors should be selected with the experience and judgment proportionate to the need. Businesses in transition need a high-functioning board.

Board Industry Market View
Typical Scenarios

Company Revenue	Fiduciary or Advisory?	Style	Recruiting Method	Talent Sourcing	Compensation	Committee Work	Time Commitment*
< $20M	Advisory	Informal	Networking	Friends & Family	Gratis or day-rate	No	A few days/year
$20M - $50M	Advisory	Semi-Formal	Mix	Friends, Consultants	Gratis or day-rate	Unlikely	4-6 days/year
$50M - $150M	Both	Mix	Mix	Consultants, Recruiters	Annual rate with expenses $20K - $50K/yr	Mix	4 - 10 days/year
$150M - $500M	Fiduciary	Formal	Traditional	Consultants, Recruiters	Annual rate with expenses $25K - $75K/yr	Yes	8 - 16 days/year

Notes
1 For private and family-owned businesses
2 Excludes start-ups, VC and PE backed entities

*Depends on committees

Figure 3

Principles For Private Company Boards

Since 1978, the Business Roundtable has issued statements on corporate governance, with the aforementioned "1997 Statement on Corporate Governance" being its seminal work. The most recent version is from 2016.

The following three quotes are the most striking takeaways from the principles that apply to private companies:

> **1. The substance of corporate governance is more important than its form; adoption of a set of rules or principles or of any particular practice or policy is not a substitute for, and does not itself assure, good corporate governance.**

Having served on private company boards and been on several *de novo* boards, private companies vary widely on what they want their boards to accomplish. Discussions about formalities that are unknown or unfamiliar distract from the more valuable work of oversight, strategy, capital structure, management readiness, and risk.

The best advice I received was to focus board discussions on a handful of existential questions that will impact the enterprise over the next three to five years.

Boards should minimize listening to reports and getting involved with non-productive group activities. Hopefully, the board will not need to manage a crisis.

If you are forming your first board, how do you know if you made the right decision? *By measuring results.* If you don't know the results you want and need, it will be difficult to know if you made the right decision.

2. Good corporate governance is not a *one-size-fits-all* proposition.

This is the second issue that stumps newer boards. No two boards are alike, nor should they be. Like a bespoke suit, it is designed and made for only one client. When designing a board, each seat should serve a specific need: marketing, finance, HR, M&A, etc. "Don't buy what you can rent" is the best mindset when selecting directors. For example, technology changes quickly, but directors don't. You can change consultants as technology changes. It is better to use board seats for knowledge and judgment that will apply over a three- to five-year horizon.

3. Providing advice and counsel to management is a key element of the board's role.

This is the punchline on what boards should do best. Where do you want and need advice and counsel? When do you want it? How do you best take advice on difficult and sensitive matters?

The tool that helps answer these questions is the board charter.

Key Elements Of A Board Charter

The charter is meant to embody the principles of good governance. The topics addressed are likely to include company history (anonymous or not), required qualifications, necessary personal characteristics, term of service, time commitment, compensation, and direction on how interested parties can apply.

This is often a synopsis of a larger piece of work on board design. A well-designed board will assign seats to specific functions or areas of expertise. These assignments are the result of vigorous discussions on priorities and what would complement the existing board members. This analysis should be based on input from ownership and to the extent practical, the management team.

Below is an example of how this may be accomplished:

The sample charter assumes this document will be posted to a public forum to solicit candidates. If the company hires a search firm, the process is similar, but there may or may not be a public posting. This communication will be more sophisticated, in the form of a prospectus or brief. A prospectus is typically a fifteen- to twenty-page descriptive document that should only be received after executing a non-disclosure agreement. This initiates the selection process.

Before the first board meeting, new members should receive a copy of the charter. These are the "rules of the road" and set expectations for how the board will operate. The sections include:

- Board Roles and Responsibilities
- Primary Duties
- Board Composition and Size
- Qualification Standards and Selection
- Board Committees
- Frequency of Board and Committee Meetings
- Content and Process of Board Meetings
- Attendance
- Term and Turnover

- Evaluation Processes
- Role of Chair and CEO
- Board Commitment
- Independence
- Change in Status and Conflicts of Interest
- Whistleblower Policy

If the company has a well-established HR policy manual and other relevant policies, they should be provided as well. Conflicts of interest and whistleblower policies are the most common examples.

Why is there so much formality? Because it helps onboard individuals who are new to the organization and creates efficiency in governance processes.

Developing Effective Board Charters

For private companies, board charters are the foundational documents that specify the board's purpose, operations, member qualifications, and expectations.

Fiduciary boards have their requirements spelled out in the bylaws. For advisory boards, the charter is likely the only document that governs their operations.

Developing Charters

So where do you start? Read as much as you can and talk to people who have the experience to provide an informed opinion. Good governance is about substance over form, and one size does not fit all.

Try something intelligent, and if it doesn't work, adapt based on the data the test produces. It is reasonable to have one board meeting to understand how it works and then change things up. That may mean changing outside advisors, refocusing the agenda, or bringing professional help so everything runs smoothly.

Good governance is a marathon, not a sprint. Be mindful to make adjustments to stay on pace.

As someone whose work is helping companies run this marathon, I find private and family-owned businesses are interesting clients. A delicate task is recommending outsiders to join a board.

When Recommending Outside Directors To Owners

As these privately owned businesses evolve, their needs change in a well-known pattern. In their early days they focus on survival, then growth, and later start to worry about continuity as they mature.

The first-generation owners are likely strong-willed entrepreneurs while the second generation is more diverse in their skills and motivation. They each have a unique personality.

Non-public businesses tend to be challenged by a lack of capital and/or a lack of talent. If they are able to overcome these issues, they grow and prosper. For the most part, if the bank is pleased and the business's taxes are current, the owners can do as they please.

This independence usually provides great satisfaction to the owners and is often a driver for why they work as hard as they do. They tend to eschew consultants and outsiders if they can avoid them. Who knows their business as well as they do?

But as the business grows and gets more complex, the owners may start to sense their own limitations. They may seek perspective or want to hear how others have dealt with their pressing issues. When this happens, leaders tend to look outside for help. After all, who can owners or CEOs talk to safely regarding existential issues? Their job is to anticipate the future and plan for it.

The primary benefits for a private company in engaging outside directors are to deal with those existential issues the owners cannot successfully resolve themselves. Even the best entrepreneurs have limitations.

Experience suggests that owners start to seek help when they deal with decisions where they may hold conflicting thoughts. This is likely because they bear up to three sets of responsibilities: as owners, board members, and management. These are different roles with distinct duties and priorities. In private and family businesses, the same people frequently hold these same three roles. If each role requires you to wear a hat, how do you know which hat to wear when? What do you do when the answers conflict?

To get a better understanding of how roles may conflict for individuals, consider using a Venn diagram to visually demonstrate the conflicts. To do this, draw three circles on a piece of paper such that they overlap in one area, while each pair of circles also overlaps. Next, label one circle each for owner, board, and management. Then write the names of individuals in each circle according to their position. This should identify how many hats each person is wearing. This is the first step to identify who should be making decisions for different issues.

The more conflict there is, the more likely the owners should consider outside directors. If you believe you should recommend that the owners bring in outside directors, how do you proceed?

Where To Start With Outside Directors

Of course, the best advice on any journey is to proceed with caution. Here are some key considerations:

Understand the marketplace. Even if the need for outside directors is compelling, inertia is a powerful force. Just because there is a clear and substantial need does not mean it will be met. The best way to overcome inertia is with education. As with many products and services, there is a market for individuals who serve as professional directors. In addition to the directors, there are consultants, search firms, and trade associations that support directors. This is a highly fragmented marketplace with diverse offerings and price points.

Each of these market participants positions itself for commercial success, has a target client profile, promotes its competitive advantage, and has a pricing model.

Understanding the marketplace puts you in a position to ask critical questions. These questions need to be asked of and answered by the controlling ownership parties. Venture capital or private equity portfolio companies are in a different marketplace than what is described here.

Define the board's mandate. For owners considering their initial board, it may be best to start by writing a board charter. As previously noted, a board charter is different from an entity's bylaws or operating agreement. The charter explains the reason the board exists, what it is expected to accomplish, and how it should function. A typical charter will cover these topics:

- Purpose and scope
- Structure (number of seats, term, committees, nominating processes)
- Meeting schedules, time commitments
- Director qualifications
- Director duties and responsibilities
- Compensation, expenses, indemnifications, insurance
- Board and director performance evaluations

Public company boards are driven by regulatory and exchange requirements. Private companies may craft their board charters more specifically to their needs. Family-owned boards are often driven by the soft issues that test a family's interpersonal relationships. Succession planning, compensation, and individual performance are usually high priorities for discussion. Financial acumen and accountability tend to follow in priority.

Understanding Liability And Defining Responsibilities

Whether the board is advisory or fiduciary, the directors should consider that they likely still bear liability. Owners should be aware of risks they are asking outsiders to accept. Family-owned businesses tend to be looking for advice and may feel more comfortable with strangers not having a legal vote on key issues. Some family businesses start with a board of advisors and evaluate if they should transition to a fiduciary board over time.

There are private companies that take the opposite view. They demand fiduciary responsibility so the outsiders have "skin in the game" to hold their attention.

As an example, a ninety-five-year-old family business formed a fiduciary board because the next generation wanted to own the business but not run it. The next generation were active professionals living in distant parts of the country. The current leadership understood they needed outside fiduciaries to hold future professional managers accountable to the family. There was significant wealth involved, and the current leaders did not want to leave it to chance that their heirs could handle that responsibility without assistance. This is essentially the same reason public companies have outside directors.

When considering the size of the board and committees, the analysis needs to go deeper. What are the performance deliverables, and how is success measured? What skills, experiences, and relationships does the board need to perform well? Most new boards are designed with each seat slotted to a specific skill set. Common slots include specific expertise in marketing, sales, ecommerce, finance, and industry or regulatory expertise. Especially when succession is an issue, some boards will have a seat slotted for a director with expertise in family succession.

The onboarding process requires forethought. Good practice will include site visits, key employee interviews, financial reviews, and corporate history and culture tutorials. Seeing the company's product in use is a high priority.

Who is best suited to help establish a new board? There is a large body of knowledge available to help with planning a new board as well as an active consulting industry that caters to this need.

The National Association of Corporate Directors is the trade association that focuses on public company boards and has an extensive library to draw upon. The Private Directors Association services only private and family-owned businesses and may be a better resource for non-public companies.

Once the planning is done and the owners have committed to proceed, a communications plan needs to be considered. Are all owners involved in the decision to proceed? If not, when do they find out? What about spouses of family executives? When and how are key employees involved? The interview process will draw attention from management and employees—who are these strangers and what are they doing here? How will it affect my job? The nature and timing of communications should be planned in advance since the owner will want to manage the message and minimize gossipy chatter.

Consider The Cost/Benefit Analysis

Because bringing in outside directors is a sensitive topic for some owners, it is worthwhile to understand the costs and benefits before making a recommendation. The typical concerns are money, time, interpersonal dynamics, and interference with the business and ownership.

What does this mean to a business looking to bring in three outside directors? It is common to hire a consultant to facilitate this process. The entire cost might be in the $100,000 to $250,000 range. Those costs will get attention.

Then compare this cost with the benefits of having a high-performing board. Do the owners have a succession plan? Are they able to resolve conflict successfully? Does their compensation system drive performance? Do they have a culture of accountability? If the answer to any of those questions is "no," what is the cost of those consequences? Are the owners likely to fix those issues without outside intervention?

While it is easier to absorb this expense at a larger company, smaller companies can find ways to initiate a board with less expense.

The time commitment to recruit and run an effective board is also significant. Assume the consultant will solicit resumes, run phone interviews, and bring forward ten finalists for three seats. Each finalist is likely to have a one-hour phone interview with an owner, maybe five finalists have a full day onsite interview, and then there may be a one-hour call with three to four of the finalists. Then there are the internal meetings to evaluate and select candidates. This summarizes the time spent facing candidates.

To get a sense of the total time required, use the consultant's rule of thumb: double the time facing the client to get the total work time required.

This quickly starts to look like an additional three to six weeks of effort to get the board seated. The board work itself could be one to three weeks of work spread over a year. For the chairperson, there is more effort to manage offline discussions in addition to preparing for and running the meetings.

Lastly, and most importantly, how does introducing outsiders change the interpersonal dynamics of the owners and key executives? How does this impact how they do their jobs today? How well will they work together? The purpose of bringing in outside directors is to effect substantial change on existential issues. This is where it is critical to understand the owners' personality and business culture.

There is the risk of perceived winners and losers. Some owners and executives will want advocates to help their cause, and others may feel threatened. If the outsiders do their job, they will quickly identify sensitive issues and force them to be constructively addressed. One common reason for an outside board is to help hold the insiders accountable, for their own benefit.

Getting Commitment And Creating Momentum

If you are an owner or executive, you already have a lot on your plate. Board establishment can be viewed as just "one more thing to do." Consider this decision as you would any other business decision. Bottom line: what is the cost/benefit?

Starting a board should be seen as a one- to three-year effort. Like any investment, you spend money and expend effort in the beginning but need time for the investment to mature and return principal and profit. New boards need time to become effective. New board members need to build relationships between themselves, owners, and management.

If board members only work together four-plus days a year, that does not create much time to build good working relationships. By design, boards grapple with existential issues, which should not be snap decisions. Some decisions will take years to bear fruit. If the board is dealing with cultural change, it may take even longer to know if the right decision was made.

Recruiting will likely be a three- to six-month process if well managed. Once candidates are committed, the onboarding process should be short and intense to get them up to speed. Good directors are bright, articulate, questioning, and eager to absorb new information. They accept the position to have an impact, and that requires them to be knowledgeable and empowered.

If you are considering starting a board, expect to spend six to twelve months of effort before holding the first formal meeting. This reinforces the logic that the owners need to be committed to the endeavor before starting.

As with all talent, director and board performance management are required once the board is seated. What if you picked the wrong person, or there was a change in circumstance once they were seated? There are a number of tools to help with director and board performance. A healthy board has a collegial environment where difficult or divisive issues can be discussed candidly. Performance is no different. As with most investments, they need to be tended to get the best results.

Focus On Planning And Execution

Determining whether to form a board with outside directors is not a simple matter. There is a marketplace for outside directors as well as an active market for the various support services the industry uses. Knowing the basics of the industry and how the service providers operate is an important step in assessing how outside directors may impact your business.

Companies start and maintain boards with independent directors to deal with their most important issues. Boards need to be effective since they are expensive, consume substantial executive time, and impact the most sensitive matters. Choosing to avoid outside directors is one way to bury difficult or unpleasant topics, but the issues do not go away.

Achieving a high-performing board with outside directors in a private company is not a simple matter. It is likely the result of a thoughtful needs assessment, a carefully crafted board mandate, meticulous recruiting and onboarding, and an unrelenting focus on director and board performance. This is a well-traveled path. Like most other subjects in business, good results depend on exemplary planning, in addition to careful execution.

What's Next

In this chapter, we focused on getting the right structure for an overall governance process, and the board's mandate. In the next chapter, we will look at finding and retaining the best people to fulfill that mandate.

Chapter 3 Takeaways

Defining The Goals Of Your Board

Define the board's mandate. A board charter is different from an entity's bylaws or operating agreement. The charter explains the reason the board exists, what it is expected to accomplish, and how it should function.

Choose the right board style. In addition to the needs of the business, the board becomes a reflection of the owners' needs and personalities.

Consider the costs/benefits. Because bringing in outside directors is a sensitive topic for some, it is worthwhile to understand the costs, benefits, and ROI before making the commitment. The typical concerns are money, time, interpersonal dynamics, and potential interference with the business and ownership.

Choose the right board type. There are three types of advisory boards: consulting, junior, and full advisory boards. They represent a scaling up of board capabilities to match the owners' and business's needs.

Build a high-performing board. Achieving a high-performing board with outside directors in a private company is not a simple matter. It requires a thoughtful needs assessment, a carefully crafted board mandate, meticulous recruiting and onboarding, and an unrelenting focus on director and board performance.

4

Recruiting And Retaining Directors And Advisors

To recruit top directors, take inspiration from the world of college football. Which head coach is the greatest recruiter of all time? If you want to start an argument, bring this up at a sports bar and you are going to hear legendary names like Bear Bryant, Lou Holtz, Nick Saban, Bobby Brown, and Urban Meyer.

According to the website Bleacher Report, one could easily make a case for Pete Carroll of USC as the top person on this list.[5]

> The run that Pete Carroll had at USC was one of, if not the greatest, runs in college football history. The Trojans not only dominated in recruiting but also on the field. Carroll was not even the third choice for USC, and many fans were furious he got the job. Reggie Bush and Matt Leinart were two of his recruits who won Heisman Trophies, while Carson Palmer won the trophy under Carroll's watch. USC had legendary talent like Shaun Cody, Len Dale White, Mark Sanchez, Dwayne Jarrett, Steve Smith, Sam Baker, Jeff Byers, Kenechi Udeze, Mike Williams, and Matt Barkley, all who signed under Carroll's recruitment.

The list of players goes on and on, as Bleacher Report notes, "Carroll got the Trojans numerous No.1 recruiting classes and stocked the roster with talent year in and year out."

As the head coach of your company, how are you going to stock your board with talent?

Attracting And Keeping Experienced Directors

Private and family-owned companies with tenured outside directors have learned how to attract, evaluate, and retain other outsider directors. Experienced directors create value by leveraging their knowledge and well-established relationships to effect change.

But where does this start? A critical step to recruiting initial directors is to understand that candidates likely lack institutional knowledge and have no meaningful relationships with current directors or the company.

Private companies seeking their initial outside directors are typically mature businesses in their second or third generation of leadership. They have experienced multiple business cycles, and the leadership is self-aware. They are looking for outsiders to fill specific needs. Often, they engage consultants to lead them through this process.

The consultants help the owners design the new board (how many directors, insiders/outsiders, candidate criteria, compensation, nominating process) and manage the selection process. The first request for resumes is typically described in a one-page anonymous summary. Once an initial phone interview is scheduled, candidates receive a two- to three-page description of the business. Sometimes they receive a marketing/sales presentation from a recent sales meeting. While useful, these documents lack context.

While this practice is sufficient to run the process, it is also one-sided. The consultants are properly focused on the needs of the owners, not the needs of the candidates. The candidates may experience a series of surprises as the discussion unfolds. How does that help to expedite the best matches? While a partner in a private equity fund, we would receive hundreds of investment summaries each year before signing non-disclosure agreements.

These teasers were usually two pages in length and told our firm what we needed to determine if we should commit resources to a project. The company summaries I have seen as a board candidate have a fraction of the content of the typical investment summary.

Candidates are deciding if they should invest a significant amount of personal time, and if they should accept reputational risk when they evaluate joining a new board. My experience suggests the selection process would be improved if it were less opaque.

Key Questions To Consider

The critical point to consider is that outside candidates for director seats frequently have little or no institutional knowledge, no sense of the company's culture, and little or no critical business data when they submit their resumes to the search committee. While the current board, owners, and their consultants are intrinsically in tune with these issues, the candidates are not. They are often recruited from different industries. Professionals seeking board seats will "opt in" until they have a reason to leave the process. Better information will accelerate the weaning process.

After reviewing a dozen searches I have been involved in, I have concluded that the following four questions need to be considered when designing the search:

What non-public data do we provide to the candidates, and when do we provide it?

This is the most difficult of the four questions since there may not be much precedent to provide guidance. Other than its bank, the company likely has not shared critical information with any outsider. The best first step is to consider "what would I want to know if it were me?" but remember the incentives are not the same.

How do we build and test relationships through the process?

Phone interviews are an effective first screen, but good relationships grow through mutual shared experiences. A good process usually includes an opening dinner with a full day of meetings the next day, including factory tours. These tours should highlight major product lines and capabilities, and provide a chance to socialize with the full management team. The more time spent together, the better they will get to know each other.

If the company is looking for multiple initial outside directors, what can it do to test the compatibility between candidates? Since the outside seats are typically slotted for specific skills, consider scheduling non-competing candidates (e.g., a finance person and a marketing person) together for onsite interviews to create interactions you can observe. I participated in this once and found it very beneficial. Meeting other candidates allows them to gauge the talent pool and get a sense of where the process is headed. I have been on boards where the initial outsiders learn of each other when they shake hands at the first meeting. That approach extends the time needed to build effective relationships.

How do we structure the recruitment process to dovetail into the onboarding process?

Plan the onboarding process first and work backward. Part of this depends on the committee structure and the interviewing that deals with committee needs (e.g., Audit, Compensation, Nominating). Matching people for committee discussions separate from the full board will expedite onboarding.

It is important to remember why outsiders serve on private boards. The reasons to serve as an outside director for a private company are (1) to have a meaningful impact on the organization, (2) to expand their network, (3) for professional growth, and for those who are at or near retirement, (4) to stay engaged. While the compensation provides respect for the time spent at meetings, it is usually not the prime motivation.

Successful professionals serve as outside directors because they want to. Over the course of a typical three-year term, there will be enough late flights, early wakeups, difficult conversations, and calendar conflicts to demotivate the candidates who are incented only by money. Better data will allow outsiders to understand their ability to have an impact and stronger relationships will motivate them to act.

Getting The Team To Gel

The typical board meets quarterly, with a few calls between meetings. Many private boards do not have formal Audit, Compensation, and Governance committees. This reduces the opportunities to work together. I have found in these situations, newcomers may need a full year to become integrated.

When soliciting candidates for initial outsider director positions, consider providing more than a few descriptive pages to brief the candidates. Most if not all of this will be revealed no later than their first board meeting. In addition to improving the interview process, you will likely receive fresh ideas to improve your business.

Once directors know each other, they will naturally start talking offline, which is the best way to build good working relationships. The goal is to have a strong, collegial environment that welcomes constructive dissent, fosters resolution, and promotes good governance. While cost is always a concern, consider inviting candidates to a few more meetings and plan tours or sales events early in their terms. Since the expected term is measured in years, amortizing these travel costs over twenty-four to thirty-six months may make it an easy decision.

Many companies purposely limit the information they provide to candidates, either from habit or due to competitive fear. The habit must disappear when the outsiders are elected, and the fear is often unjustified. Providing timely, critical datasets and multiple opportunities to build personal relationships are critical to selecting and onboarding the best outside directors. It is a learning process for the owners, frequently more so than for the candidates.

Designing Your First Private Company Board Of Directors

Many private companies under $100 million in revenue do not have outside directors for a variety of reasons. I find owners tend to consider bringing in outside directors when they "get stuck" on issues that require the experience and judgment they lack. When owners find themselves in this situation, they often don't know what questions to ask.

So here is a list of the major decisions to address when your governance needs start to evolve. The logic behind the answers is important, as it will shape how the board is formed, how it functions, and its ultimate impact on the business.

What are the major issues to address during the next three to five years?

Effective boards have clear mandates. What is the board expected to accomplish and what dates or milestones are important to understand? Are you concerned with industry disruption? Succession planning? Are there specific financial goals to achieve? Board discussions should have deep strategic content.

Most private companies use advisory boards, which means outsiders tend to be excluded from certain sensitive issues (e.g., executive compensation, CEO performance appraisals, ownership distributions, and succession planning). Outsiders will want to understand this to assess their level of interest in possibly joining a younger board.

How will you measure the board's success?

Boards that don't evaluate their performance are more likely to underperform. How will you evaluate and provide feedback to the board as a whole and its individual members? How will they know if they are successful? Good outside directors will ask about your evaluation methods during the interview process.

Should it be an advisory or fiduciary board?

Many private companies still use advisory boards, often because the owners are not ready to have outsiders control a portion of their destiny. Owners may look to avoid the expense of D&O liability insurance if they can. The way I see it, good outside advisors understand having their voice heard is likely more important than casting a vote.

Advisory boards are often viewed as the first evolutionary step toward a full fiduciary board. When a family wants to retain ownership of its business, but the kids don't want to run it, a fiduciary board is warranted.

What are the real and potential conflicts?

Part of this analysis requires identifying existing and potential conflicts. Candidates will want to know what they are walking into. What are the big risks a new advisor/director will need to address? What are the family squabbles that impact the business? Did a key executive leave or cause a reputational problem? Are there pending lawsuits or regulatory issues?

These issues need to be identified, not solved, when forming a board. This is the time to review the indemnifications included in the bylaws as well as the need for D&O insurance.

How will you determine the board's composition and operations?

How many seats in total are planned, and what types of expertise do they represent? As previously noted, each outsider seat is typically filled with a specific expertise that cannot be "rented" via consultants. These seats are scarce, so they should be assigned wisely.

Who really needs to be in the room, and do they need a vote or not? If the board is stacked with insiders, it may be harder to secure competent outsiders.

How long do terms last, and are they staggered?

While one year and three years are typical terms, those are not magic numbers. How long does it take for individual members to become experienced and effective yet still remain fresh? My experience is that de novo boards need a full year to become effective. The members will only have a few hours per quarter to develop their working relationships.

Who will be chair and why?

Is it a formality, or is this the person who really sets and manages the agenda, assigns committees, and runs the meetings? The owner of the business may be better served by not being the chair, so they can be more engaged in the discussion. An outside lead director or a non-executive chair may be beneficial to consider.

How many meetings per year are expected?

In addition, how long should they be and are they in person or virtual? COVID-19 changed how boards worked, just like most everything else. That said, in-person meetings are often more effective since a virtual experience takes away the nonverbal communications that only happen when you are face to face.

While four full-day meetings per year are typical, that may be irrelevant to your situation. The goal is to make the meeting effective and advance the business, not fill time. A well-run four-hour meeting is better than an eight-hour slog.

What are your budget and timeline?

A board is a business function, just like marketing, sales, and operations. It needs to have a clear mandate, performance metrics, and budget.

Expenses include the one-time costs to form the board and recruit candidates as well as the annual costs of compensation and travel. De novo boards may need three to nine months to get to a first meeting, depending on their success at recruiting new members and scheduling difficulties.

Businesses should design their governance mechanisms based on a thorough analysis of the ownership group's needs and the specifics of the business.

A separate subject is how to position the business to be attractive to candidates. Outsiders will want to have a good sense of the situation before they start the interview process. Things they will likely want to know about early on include the business's competitive position, financial health, growth prospects, ownership and succession plans, as well as the competence of its management.

Good governance is an art more than a science, and it takes time and good judgment to keep its mechanisms tuned to the ever-changing needs of ownership and the business.

In practicing good governance, there are six lessons I often share with privately owned businesses.

Six Lessons When Forming New Boards Of Directors

As I look back at the many new boards I have been involved in organizing, certain lessons keep repeating. While there are nuanced differences between fiduciary and advisory boards, the basics are the same. In my experience, advisory boards tend to have a narrower scope than fiduciary boards. They mostly pertain to private, not public companies, and they are rarely responsible for regulatory issues.

If you are thinking about forming a new board, keep these lessons in mind:

Lesson one: Establishing a board is a process, not a quick event. Getting to the first meeting likely requires six to nine months or more. This time is used to draft a charter; define qualifications, personal characteristics, experience, and other factors; build a pool of competitive candidates; and run the interview process. Most processes require multiple rounds of interviews to narrow the pool to only the worthiest candidates. Remember, "fit" is the single most important factor in board member selection and success.

Getting the new board to become a cohesive decision-making body typically requires a year of operation. If they only spend four days a year working together, that is not much time to get to know one another and develop trust. Active committees do help in this regard. I find the best onboarding process includes one-to-one time between all combinations of internal and outside board members starting as soon as elections are confirmed.

Lesson two: Understand the constituencies. The board's mandate and its members need to be focused on the needs of their constituencies. While this is mandated as ownership, the word "stakeholder" is commonly used for good reasons. The board needs to understand preexisting conflicts and how they came to be. Directors need to understand where stakeholders may hinder progress or outright sabotage needed changes. These understandings become the foundation for the judgment and perspective they will need to guide the organization forward.

Lesson three: Deliver a clear mandate. You should form a board to advise the ownership on critical questions. These few questions should anticipate the major issues that are likely to occur during the next three to five years. It is too late for a new board to address today's problems. Consultants are likely better suited to resolve immediate needs. The individuals driving the board formation process need to devote time for quiet reflection and deep conversations to anticipate the future and the requisite organizational challenges that are likely to occur.

Lesson four: Manage the outsiders. Don't be afraid to change players in the middle of the game. Sometimes a candidate presents well and interviews well but doesn't fit in with everyone else. A sophisticated recruiting process will consider how the leading candidates will mesh. Strong candidates will want to know who they are dealing with before they commit to a one- or three-year term of service.

Lesson five: Include the management team. The top tier of management that is not on the board is a critical support function for the board's deliberations. Best practices suggest having these functional leaders meet and present to the board on a rotating basis. Board members want to hear from the people who do the work. This is an easy means to check on what they are being told by the CEO and/or CFO who funnel and sanitize most of the information they receive. This also helps the outside board members understand the company's culture. It will make the managers feel better by taking away the mystery of the boardroom.

Lesson six: Evaluate and inform. Feedback is the breakfast of champions. Board evaluations are a process unto themselves. For instance, will you have group or individual reviews? Will you conduct surveys or interviews? Who, how, and when is the feedback delivered? How will you deal with a negative review? Evaluations can help improve board performance but need to be done thoughtfully. Frankly, I believe this only becomes relevant after a few years of operation; at that point, the chairperson can understand the group's dynamics and decide how to navigate this delicate issue.

Boards often make all the difference when it comes to business performance, succession planning, and risk management. While each situation is unique, the process to launch a new board is fairly well understood. It makes sense to learn from the past.

A question I am often asked is how to assess candidates who will make good members of an advisory board.

How To Assess Candidates

Over the years, I have worked with numerous companies looking to form their first board of advisors or fiduciary board of directors. This issue often comes up as revenues approach the $25 million to $30 million range—the point where companies tend to hit a wall that forces owners to look for help.

I believe this is due to the theory of span of control. In management, the traditional theory is that one manager can effectively manage five to eight people. As technology has changed how we work, the new theory is that a manager can handle up to fifteen to twenty subordinates effectively. The truth likely falls in the middle.

The board corollary of this theory is that owners and management both hit their limits when they lack the experience to address new challenges. Growth creates new problems to solve and changes the context of decision-making. The problems are larger and more complex, the risk of errors increases, and self-confidence is challenged. When you aren't sure what to do, it is time to ask for help.

Think about what else changes as you grow your business: You need a bigger bank, you need more capital to fund growth, hiring key talent becomes more expensive, and there is more to delegate. Running a business simply gets more complicated with success.

If you are going to bring in outside voices, what voices should be heard, and how do you qualify them? What is the process you intend to use to fill these newly created board seats? Here is a breakdown of four key steps I believe should be part of this process.

Step one: Identify ownership priorities and needs. Start by identifying your ownership goals and assessing what it will take to get there. What do you want the business to achieve over the next five years? Set specific benchmarks for revenue, profits, valuations, and the health of the balance sheet. Now develop the business strategy that will get you there.

Then run the gap analysis: We know what we need, and we know what we have, so what is missing? This should speak to functional and industry expertise. You are trying to define candidate profiles for people you want in a long-term business relationship. Don't buy skills you can rent, especially if the field is changing rapidly. While the number one priority for recruiting board members is fit, you need to build the profile analytically from the ground up.

Depending on your approach, you may receive one hundred resumes for each posting or more. You need objective criteria to cull candidates to create a manageable list.

Step two: Assess industry dynamics. The second issue to consider is your industry situation. Is it static or dynamic? How fast is it growing? Has it been or is it likely to be disrupted? Do you intend to be the disruptor, or are you playing catch-up? How are you positioned, and is that where you want or need to be?

After considering functional and industry expertise, think about change management experience. Managing change through internal and external processes is about experience. If you are bracing for a storm, it helps to have a captain and crew who have been through a few hurricanes before.

Specific topics to evaluate include new competitors or suppliers, substitute products, technology, regulations, supply chain, talent, and costs.

Obviously, this means looking into the future and making a call on what is going to happen to your industry. If your management team doesn't have an informed opinion or you are unsettled about it, you have more work to do to understand your likely future.

Step three: Consider your management team. The third piece of the puzzle is your future management needs and expectations. Does your team function as a well-oiled machine, or does it need a tune-up? Has it demonstrated experience and judgment commensurate with the current and future needs of the business? Would some managers benefit from mentoring while others should be left alone?

These questions should not be evaluated at a single point in time but rather considered with the next three to five years in mind. Developing a strong management team is a process, not an event. You may need to make a few trades along the way. You need the right talent and experience, and you need managers who work together effectively. What do you need from your board to make this happen now?

Step four: Examine risk management. The last piece of the puzzle, risk management, requires special attention. This tends to get overlooked by management and ownership, but it is the issue that most determines future success. Most teams do not spend much time assessing risk in a systematic manner, by which I mean the uninsurable risks hiding in plain sight.

One very striking feature of private companies is that owners will accept risks in their business that they would not accept elsewhere. After decades of running a business, you get comfortable accepting the things you can't change. But this is a bad habit because these risks tend to become major issues for due diligence during transactions. I have seen owners surprised by how much attention a buyer spends on an issue the owner never thinks about.

The Art Of Designing A Board

Because even a full board cannot include every conceivable skill and expertise, selecting the best possible board is an art. This requires establishing the seats you need to fill first, then recruiting the best fit candidates. Sometimes, CEOs become enamored with a personality first, then try to fit that personality on the board; these scenarios rarely result in long-term success.

Board members must be able to maintain objectivity in all circumstances; this is their primary responsibility. Your board will quickly lose its effectiveness if members cannot offer their honest opinions. A good board member is able to tactfully disagree with ownership and offer alternative solutions without fear of being replaced. They have mastered the art of disagreeing without being disagreeable.

Though assembling a board requires careful thought and insight, there is a relatively simple litmus test for its sustainability: in a well-functioning board, colleagues are able to have a visceral disagreement, then immediately look forward to going out to lunch with each other.

Bringing It All Together

A skills matrix is the tool to bring these ideas all together onto one piece of paper. The columns should be the candidates being considered for the board, while the rows should identify the function, industry expertise, and business development skills that are needed. The industry dynamics and management team needs will drive the prioritization of these factors.

Skills	Importance To Board	\multicolumn{9}{c	}{Directors}
	Board	#1	#2	#3	#4	#5	#6	#7	#8	New Director
Industry Expertise	A	A	B	C	B	C	C	C	C	A
Manufacturing Industry	A	A	A	A	A	A	C	A	A	
CEO/COO/B.U. President	A	A	A	A	A	A	C	A	C	A
Operations	B	C	A	A	A	A	B	B	B	B
Strategy & Planning	B	B	B	A	A	A	A	A	B	
Governance	A	C	B	A	B	B	A	A	B	
International	A	A	B	B	A	A	B	A	A	A
M & A	A	C	C	B	B	C	A	A	A	
Marketing & Sales	B	A	B	B	B	A	B	A	C	
Financing	B	B	B	C	B	B	A	B	A	
Accounting & Reporting	B	C	B	C	C	C	C	B	A	
Legal & Regulatory	C	C	C	C	C	C	C	C	B	
IT	C	C	C	C	C	A	C	C	A	
IR/PR	C	C	C	C	C	C	A	C	B	
HR	C	C	C	A	B	B	B	B	B	B

Legend
A - Significant Experience
B - Moderate Experience
C - Modest Experience/familiarity

Figure 4

This matrix is a useful tool to enumerate the needs within the boardroom and match candidates with your priorities. While the outcome looks simple, it incorporates a great deal of thought and judgment that will help you choose your board confidently.

What's Next

At this point, you might be convinced that advice is a good idea but wonder if it is a good investment. Of course, the wise action to take is to count the cost, which is examined in the next chapter.

Chapter 4 Takeaways

Recruiting And Retaining Directors And Advisors

Realize that establishing a board is a process, not an event. Getting to the first meeting may require six to nine months or longer. This time is used to draft a charter; define candidate qualifications; build a pool of competitive candidates; run the interview process; select and then onboard the candidates.

Think long-term. Getting the new board to become a cohesive decision-making body typically requires a year of operation. If they only spend four days a year working together, that is not much time to get to know one another and develop trust. Active committees do help in this regard.

Understand the constituencies. The board's mandate and its members need to be focused on the needs of their constituencies. While this is generally understood as ownership, the word "stakeholder" is commonly used for good reasons.

Deliver a clear mandate. You should form a board to advise the ownership on critical questions. These few questions should anticipate the major issues that are likely to occur during the next three to five years.

Manage the players. Don't be afraid to change players in the middle of the game. Sometimes a candidate presents and interviews well but doesn't fit in with everyone else.

Include the management team. The top tier of management that is not on the board may provide critical support for the board's deliberations. It helps to have these functional leaders present to the board on a rotating basis.

5

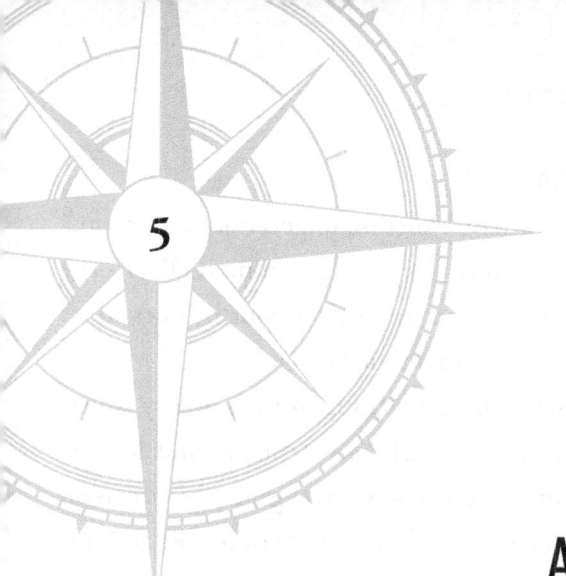

Costs Of A Board And Compensation

Is a board a good bet for your business?

Speaking of betting, that is an activity that is on the rise. An estimated sixty-eight million Americans placed a wager on the NCAA's annual March Madness basketball tournament in 2023, up from forty-five million in 2022, according to the American Gaming Association.[6]

The gaming association drew its estimates from an online survey of 2,200 adults. By comparison, an estimated fifty million placed some kind of bet on Super Bowl LVII in 2023. That translates to about 25 percent of the adult population.

But 100 percent of privately owned companies wager on their businesses every month of the year, only they call those wagers investments in people.

You need to bet on great people if you want to accomplish great things.

"At the end of the day, you bet on people, not strategies," said Lawrence Bossidy, former CEO at AlliedSignal (later Honeywell).

Whether for a small startup or a decades-old family business, betting on a group of advisors can help fill management's gaps in expertise. But that help comes with an investment.

Noses In, Fingers Out, Sensors On

Great directors operate with the motto of "noses in, fingers out, sensors on."

If you have a board of directors, how do you determine its ROI? The benefits tend to be intangible but the costs are real. If your business does not have a board, creating one may be a dramatic change.

Highly effective private company boards focus their time on key issues. Using one more sports analogy, boards have playbooks for offense and defense.

Offensive plays include developing effective strategy, engaging in succession planning, and managing capital. Defensive plays include oversight and risk management.

Public boards have these same priorities in addition to broader responsibilities set by their regulators.

A high-performing board helps management formulate and execute a strategy to achieve the owner's objectives. Many private businesses lack this kind of formal planning process.

Outside directors can bring a systematic approach to developing business strategy, allocating resources, and providing accountability. Outsiders typically bring relationships to help deploy the strategy. As noted previously, a common reality with private companies is that as long as the bank and the taxman are happy, it's easy to become complacent. But if the owners are committed to growth, the directors should be working to make it happen.

With a reasonable multiple, this additional growth should be worth significant value. It is common for owners to look for a 10 to 25 percent increase in value, depending on their opportunity set.

How does this increase compare to the cash costs of running the board?

How Much Are Private Company Board Directors Compensated?

There is an active and well-established market for private and public company directors. While a public company's board director compensation is transparent, the same is not true for private companies.

There are a number of sources for private company board compensation data, which tends to be grouped into segments based on revenue ranges of the businesses involved.

Let's take a deep dive into director compensation.

Average Compensation For The Board of Directors

The market segments by company revenue size. Below is what I usually suggest as appropriate board compensation to owners forming a new board, based on company revenue size:

- **Under $20 million.** Private companies under $20 million in revenue tend not to have boards, and if they do they are informal advisory boards. There tends to be little compensation, as these are "golf buddies" and not traditional, independent outside directors.
- **$20 million–$50 million.** These businesses are starting to form advisory boards with a semblance of normalized function, although many are "consulting boards" and not yet advisory boards. Compensation here tends to be a day rate for professional time.
- **$50 million–$200 million.** These boards tend to be true advisory boards, with regular schedules, agendas, and meaningful structure. Compensation is typically in the $20,000 to $30,000 per year range and may be structured several different ways.
- **Above $200 million.** Compensation increases to the $25,000 to $75,000 per year range, with a wider variation in structure and total compensation. The majority of these boards are fiduciary.

These figures exclude PE portfolio companies, which tend to pay much more, and VC businesses, which tend not to pay cash compensation to directors—most of whom are typically insiders.

During my tenure as chairman of Director Development and Training at the Private Directors Association, I saw postings for about fifty seats per year. To the extent compensation was listed in a posting, the data was generally consistent with these rules of thumb.

Survey On Director Pay

A 2020 study of director compensation was published by *Private Company Director Magazine*, along with Compensation Advisory Partners and *Family Business Magazine*.[7] The initial study was published in 2019.

The 2020 study included 982 respondents. (Updated studies are available online.) About 60 percent of the respondents were under $100 million in revenue, and another 20 percent were greater than $250 million in revenue. The vast majority of the respondents were family businesses, with the balance being mainly privately controlled entities.

Here are some aspects to consider:

Median board retainer. Based on the data, the median board retainer by revenue is consistent with my past observations, with the overall median coming in at $28,000 per year, down slightly from 2019. Contrary to prior observations, companies under $50 million revenue were paying $20,000 in annual compensation. That is one benefit of a larger dataset and a statistically valid approach as compared to general observation.

Cash compensation was a combination of annual retainers and meeting fees. The public company practice of paying only via retainers is starting to be embraced by private companies, as meeting fees continue to decrease as a percentage of total compensation.

Additional findings. Not more than 25 percent of the respondents used some form of long-term compensation, which was mainly equity-based for those that did.

Independent lead directors and board chairs earn an additional $13,200 to $20,000 per year, while committee chairs are often paid an additional $5,000 per year. Board size has increased from 2019, up to six to ten with a median of eight directors seated.

Diversity in the boardroom is increasingly more important, and I expect that trend will need more time to be truly impactful.

My observations presented above are not scientific but good approximations to help owners understand how and how much a board director is paid. The survey is statistically robust, and fortunately corroborates my unscientific observations.

Other Resources On Director Compensation

There are a number of other compensation studies available. Many are behind website paywalls. Here are some of the more well-known sources:

Lodestone Global has been publishing private company board compensation studies since 2013, which are available online.

The National Association of Corporate Directors (NACD) also has compensation studies for public and private companies that are behind its paywall.

A number of search firms have their own private databases that they use in recommending compensation to clients. These reports are for North American businesses. There are separate datasets for businesses located in Europe, such as Nurole.

Board Compensation Should Match Board Performance

While these thoughts summarize private company board compensation, they should be viewed as half of the equation. The other—and more important—half of this issue is board performance.

What are you getting for the compensation? To obtain the best results, the two need to be tied together. The board is a business expense made by the owner to enhance their investment, just as with all other business functions. It needs to be evaluated and be held accountable to get the best results. Regardless of what you pay, make sure you are getting full value for your investment.

That's right, invest, not spend. Governance is a business investment, and the ROI should be measured like any investment.

Successful firms view their boards of directors as competitive weapons.

Boards influence the most important business matters. And since they are expensive and consume substantial time, a board of directors' involvement needs to be effective.

When properly constructed and thoughtfully led, boards of directors create significant value for shareholders. Boards should focus on high-impact matters, including:

- Oversight
- Strategy
- Succession planning
- Capital structure
- Risk management

Choosing to avoid formal governance structures is a popular way to bury nonperformance and other unpleasant topics. But these problems don't go away on their own.

The Costs Of Acquiring A Board Of Directors

Some private companies have effective boards with no outsiders, but that is less common. Typically, outsiders drive effective governance. The primary concerns when bringing in outside directors are:

1. Cost
2. Time
3. Interpersonal dynamics.

What does this mean to a company considering bringing in three outside directors?

It is common to hire a consultant to facilitate this process. The cost to have a consultant help form the board and operate it for one year (assuming four onsite meetings plus travel) may be $100,000 to $250,000—depending on a variety of assumptions.

The time commitment to recruit and run an effective board is significant. Even if the owner hires a board consultant, reaching the first meeting may total four to eight months of effort. The board work itself could be one to three weeks of work, spread over a year.

For the chairperson, managing offline discussions requires more work—as well as preparing for and running the meetings. Board members must always be aware about how their decisions impact executive deliverables.

Lastly—and maybe most importantly—how do outsiders change the interpersonal dynamics of the owner and key executives? How well will they work together? The purpose of bringing in outside directors is to effect substantial change. Management will have concerns about how outsiders impact their careers.

This is why experienced directors say, "it is all about fit."

What Is The ROI Of Your Board?

Author Brené Brown once said, "I believe that feedback thrives in cultures where the goal is not 'getting comfortable with hard conversations' but 'normalizing discomfort.'"[8]

Feedback can cause discomfort.

It is true for boards as well as most other business functions. Thoughtful board evaluations are the best way to achieve a high ROI from a board. An evaluation may be performed on the board as a unit and/or individual board members. There are numerous techniques to accomplish this delicate task.

There is a well-established market of board consultants who will design and execute a board evaluation process tailored to your circumstances.

Structuring The Board Evaluation Process

There are several key questions to address when considering board evaluations.

What is the goal of the evaluation? A new board needs time to evolve to achieve its full effectiveness, and feedback is a quick way to see where it needs to grow. A mature board will have well-defined processes to be evaluated and needs to think about how to stay fresh.

Who is participating in the evaluation? Board evaluations should include board members, key non-board executives, and outside ownership. If conditions require, there could be other stakeholders who need to be heard.

Who should conduct the evaluation? This usually falls to the chairperson, outside counsel, or a consultant. All participants must trust the facilitator. If the intention is to give individual feedback to board members, the leader needs to have the tact and gravitas to deliver feedback so it is accepted.

What is the best methodology for evaluation? The typical methods include questionnaires and personal interviews. The design of each is critical, but there are ample tools available to consider. An informal approach may be best the first time through. Like most board processes, they evolve over time.

There are numerous in-depth surveys regarding director compensation, but there is little or no reviewed data on private company board evaluations. Based on hearsay, I estimate that less than 15 percent of private company boards use a formal evaluation process on a routine basis. However, there always seems to be time to do this on an ad hoc basis after a crisis.

The decision to conduct an evaluation and how the results are used is a measure of the quality of the ownership of the business. Good owners will drive continuous improvement at all levels of the business, including the board. They want to know the IRR of their investment in the board as much as they would any other investment.

The toughest decisions in business lack formulas that neatly provide answers. Developing a high-performing board that creates substantial value is not a simple matter. It takes judgment to value intangible benefits against hard costs.

The ROI is a series of seamlessly linked and well-executed processes:

- Formal needs assessment
- Critical structuring
- Thoughtful recruiting and onboarding
- An unrelenting focus on director and board performance

This is a path well-traveled. The value of a high-performing board is obvious when the process is well managed.

What's Next

Having great board members who are fairly compensated is not enough to assure effective meetings. In the next chapter, we will examine what the chair needs to do to make sure board members deliver meaningful results.

Chapter 5 Takeaways

Costs Of A Board And Compensation

Focus on strategy. A high-performing board helps management formulate and execute a strategy to achieve the owner's objectives. This often drives the ROI of the board. Many private businesses lack this kind of formal planning process.

Outside directors bring a great deal. Outside directors can bring a systematic approach to developing business strategy, allocating resources, and providing accountability. Outsiders may bring relationships to help deploy the strategy.

For companies under $20 million. Private companies under $20 million in revenue tend not to have boards, and if they do, they are informal advisory boards. There tends to be little compensation, as these are "golf buddies" and not traditional, independent outside directors.

For companies in the $20 million–$50 million range. These businesses are starting to form advisory boards with a semblance of normalized function, although many are "consulting boards" and not yet advisory boards. Compensation here tends to be a day rate for professional time.

For companies in the $50 million–$200 million range. These boards tend to be true advisory boards, with regular schedules, agendas, and meaningful structure. Compensation is typically in the $20,000 to $30,000 per year range and may be structured several different ways.

For companies above $200 million. Compensation increases to the $25,000 to $75,000 per year range, with a wider variation in structure and total compensation. Many of these boards are fiduciary.

Feedback can cause discomfort. It is true for boards as well as for people. Thoughtful board evaluations are the best way to achieve a high ROI from a board. An evaluation may be performed on the board as a unit and/or individual board members. There are numerous techniques to accomplish this delicate task.

6

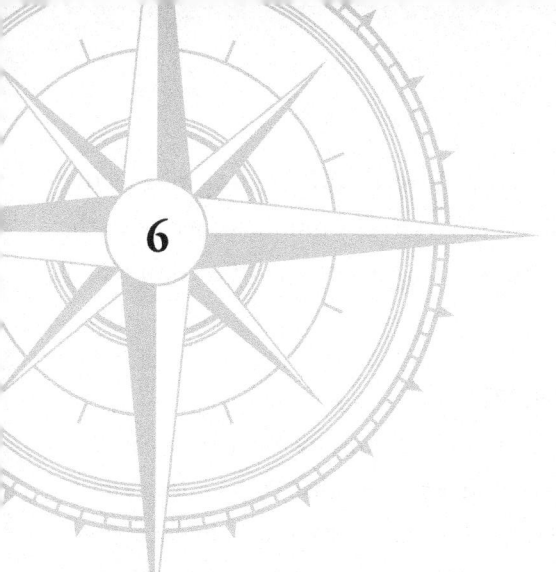

Planning Effective Board Meetings

Your business has a chain of command, an idea that dates back to the Roman Empire.

Consider this excerpt from an essay published by the U.S. Army War College:

> *Without a doubt, the chain of command is one of the most durable concepts in military organizations. From Roman times until present, the chain of command fixed formal authorities and accountability from the highest leader to the front-line soldier. It made the generation, issuing, and following of orders simple despite the vastness of formations being put to battle. The chain also formalized the separation of officers and soldiers into different castes. As societies industrialized, formal chains of command were instituted in bureaucracy which would become the leading model of organization in the civilian sector.*[9]

But a board is outside the chain of command. A board is designed to push back and hold accountable the forces of authority.

Employees are expected to follow the directions they are given. Boards are designed to question those directions to generate better outcomes.

The chair of the board of directors is charged with creating an effective board meeting agenda. A board of directors serves a unique function in the business world and behaves differently from most parts of a commercial organization.

Who Sets The Board Meeting Agenda?

The chairperson usually sets the agenda and controls the board's impact and effectiveness. The agenda needs to consider what to discuss and decisions to be made. It will also address gathering information to productively manage decision-making. Allocating an appropriate amount of time for each topic means the difference between a fruitful meeting and a waste of time.

Boards are responsible for five concepts:

- Oversight
- Strategy
- Capital
- Management succession
- Risk management

The chair needs to know how to juggle these matters so the board can do its job and do it well.

What Makes An Effective Board Meeting Agenda?

Get direction from ownership—what do they want the board to accomplish? Boards are the bridge between ownership and management. The person setting the agenda needs to understand what ownership expects from the board. For long-tenured boards, this is not a common concern. For newer boards, especially with smaller companies, this is frequently a material issue.

The issue starts with this thought: "I think I need a board but I am not sure what they can do for me." If ownership doesn't know what it wants, then someone—usually an experienced outsider—needs to step in to fill the leadership void.

The value owners receive from their boards depends on the questions they ask of them. If you ask targeted, pointed questions, you are likely to get more from the board. When preparing an agenda, it's important to find out what is on participants' minds. If your questions require technical expertise not available via board members, an outside consultant may be the answer. Then the board is responsible for applying judgment based on the consultant's input.

Stay Focused On Future Issues

There is a human bias to focusing on the *crisis du jour* (the crisis of the day). Of course, immediate issues need to be addressed. However, the primary purpose of a board of directors is to anticipate issues several years ahead and develop ways to overcome or take advantage of each scenario. Most strategic board discussions focus on planning and management succession.

This is why when preparing an agenda, it is helpful to ask the participants what, if anything, is on their minds that should be discussed.

Consider these actions:

Maintain an annual cycle of evergreen topics. Certain subjects need to be addressed every year, and it is beneficial to spread them out over twelve months to make meetings more manageable. Examples include strategy development, budgets, succession planning, performance evaluations, compensation, and risk management.

Minimize reporting, maximize discussion, and improve decision-making time. Board time is precious. It should not be wasted on reporting that can be done through pre-reads and ancillary conversations. Deliver the board book far enough in advance so participants can read it, consider it, and prepare questions. Experienced chairs know things change, even with a well-designed board meeting agenda. Sometimes entire agendas need to shift in the middle of a meeting if conversations shed light on unforeseen issues. However, by knowing the room, learning how participants take in information, and recognizing how decisions are made, you may be able to rewrite the agenda on the fly.

Bring in key managers who would not otherwise interact with the board. The board can get a better feel for what is happening on the ground if they meet with lower-level managers from time to time. This kind of practice provides engagement without interfering with management. Meetings should be a thoughtful part of leadership development. Management can identify up and comers and give them exposure to the board as part of their individual development plan. If there are multiple meeting locations, it is common to rotate meetings across them to give the board and local management exposure to each other.

Make time for self-evaluation. Effective board meeting agendas reserve time for the board to evaluate itself. Board evaluations are complex and essential to board performance; at least annually, it's important to include time on the agenda. Some boards set evaluation summary and discussion time outside regular meetings.

Understand an effective board meeting agenda requires planning. Most people don't think about how a board meeting agenda is created or what goes into it. Board members are likely to find the agenda in their email and simply react. But planning ahead is a vital element in having an effective board and effective board meetings. The most desirable outcomes happen when a deliberate, useful board meeting agenda addresses key issues and is presented in advance with enough data to facilitate decisions. An effective preparer allows adequate time per subject so as to permit thoughtful deliberations and conclusions.

The following are templates to help you prepare for board meetings:

Board of Directors Meeting
Date
AGENDA

I. Call to Order, Welcome and Announcements – *Chairman*   (XX minutes)

II. Consent Agenda – Chairman   (XX minutes)
    1. Questions about distributed materials
        a. Minutes of prior Board of Directors Meeting
        b. Financials
        c. Distributed Reports
    2. Motion to accept the Consent Agenda

III. Management Presentation & Discussion   (XX minutes)
    a. Division ABC
    b. Division XYZ

IV. CEO Report & Discussion   (XX minutes)

V. Standing Committee Reports   (XX minutes)
    a. Audit Committee
    b. Compensation Committee
    c. Nominating and Governance Committee
    d. Risk Committee
    e. Ethics Committee

VI. Action Items Status Report from Previous Board Meeting   (XX minutes)

VII. Motions for approval – *Chairman*   (XX minutes)

VIII. Other Business   (XX minutes)
    a. Open discussion
    b. Next meeting date

IX. Adjournment

X. Executive Session – *Independent Directors*

Board Meeting Minutes

Acme Inc.
Board of Advisors Meeting Notes
July 12, 2022

Topic: Business Update
Outcome:
Update the Board on current business results and outlook.
Solicit advice and perspective on key business initiatives.

Summary notes:
- International—on the brink of a decision—hopefully by end of year.
  - Lots of people changes, some large corporate accounts coming on board.
  - Need to set a timetable and a set of criteria for making a decision.
  - Is the issue fundamentals or leadership?
- Recruitment and Turnover—look at a 4-box analysis of what's triggered by organization, what by external environment, what by personal life, and what by work experience. See if can find some generalities to review.
- Supply chain—we are in good shape.
- Outbound freight increased costs—we are not adding a surcharge, just raising pricing. Inbound container suppliers aren't lowering contract prices, but spot prices dropping.
- Next price raise will be regular annual one in August 2023.

Action items:

Who	What	By When
Steve	Define timetable and criteria for international decision	End January
Alice	Review how other companies are changing recruiting efforts given market dynamics	End September

Topic: Strategy Five-Year Plan
Outcome:
Review the five-year plan draft – get specific feedback on content, activation and whether there is an appropriate level of stretch in the goals.

Summary notes:
- How do we activate the road map? Exec meeting on 7/14 was intended to do that.
- How can we hold the Exec accountable to be clear and specific on what they are going to stop doing?
- Inflation so far has had about a 3 percent impact on this year's growth—do we want to adjust our targets to exclude inflation?
- What new capabilities do we need to build to achieve vision? How will we identify? What are specifics we will want to develop around the next vertical?
- What do we need to do to support revenue?
- Should we be doing any sensitivity analysis on costs that are out of our control? Labor? Medical? What are the most impactful top three uncontrollable expense items?
- Inventory control issues—especially one customer styles.
- Do we need some dedicated resources to address continuous improvement opportunities?
- What's our level of succession readiness for top thirty critical positions?

Action items:

Who	What	By When
John	Look at private equity offerings to see if we are in the right range for expenses	End August
Bob	Establish a quarterly mechanism to review company-wide initiatives and priorities and check the resource allocation/feasibility of execution	End Sept
John/ Sue	Consider sensitivity analysis for top three expense items – build mitigation actions if warranted	End Sept
Robin	Inventory control – build and embed specific process for managing inventory and controlling SKU proliferation	TBD
Irene	Build linkage from strategy to broader capability planning efforts	Build into yearly strategic planning/ operating cycle
Sue	Ensure talent management process embeds top player review and includes a form of retention assessment	Timing to link to yearly talent planning cycle

Topic: Elevating The Board
Outcome:
Discuss how we might continue to evolve the board and increase its impact over time.

Summary notes:
- What is the ninety-day succession plan if something happens to CEO?
- What uninsurable risks are we exposed to?
- What are the owners' expectations of what is needed from board—we should clarify this and then review performance based on this set of expectations.
- Given strategy—what are the top three or four org capabilities that we need to develop?
    - Process
    - Technology
    - People

Acme Inc. Board Action Items
9/8/22 Board Meeting Results

ID #	Date Initiated	Action Item	Responsible Party	Status Update	Original Target Completion Date
1	6/9/22	Establish a Line of Credit	Terry	9/8 LOC authorized by bank	11/18/22
2	6/9/22	Submit Org Dev Proposal	Susan	First version submitted 8/17/22. Bill to revise per Board direction. Bill already finished Phase I of the proposal.	Completed
3	6/9/22	Develop Performance Incentive System	Karen	Gary working with Susan & John on an incentive program for the Service Center.	12/5/22
4	6/9/22	Develop a Marketing Plan	Susan	Have decided to hire a Marketing Director	4/23/23
5	6/9/22	Complete Product Planning	Doug		
6	9/8/22	Hire Warehouse Consultant	Karen	Interviewing candidates complete, reviewing proposals. Expect decision in next 2 weeks.	12/1/22
7	9/8/22	Develop a Wish List for Sales Support	Carla	Need the standard marketing material: Brochures, New Product Announcements, etc. Waiting for Marketing Director	4/2023
8	9/8/22	Build Data Lake	Carla	This is very low on the priority list.	Take off the list of action items
9	9/8/22	Develop New Branding Program	Peter	Peter and Kyle will need to work with our Marketing Manager when hired.	4/2023
10	9/8/22	Product Quality Analysis	Sam	Orders placed with the factory	Completed
11	9/8/22	Consignment Inventory	Doug	Factory A complete; Factories B and C started	Partially complete
12	9/8/22	Hire Executive Search Firm	Karen	Have changed direction, No search firm required.	Not Required

What Comes Next

Much of the real work of the board is done on the committee level. In the next chapter, we examine the three most important committees and how they work together to produce superior governance results.

Chapter 6 Takeaways

Planning Effective Board Meetings

A board is outside the chain of command. A board is designed to push back and hold accountable the forces of authority. Employees are expected to follow the directions they are given. Boards are designed to question those directions to generate better outcomes.

An effective board meeting agenda requires planning. Most people don't think about how a board meeting agenda is created or about what goes into it. But planning ahead is a vital element in having an effective board and productive board meetings. This is the chairperson's responsibility.

Minimize reporting, maximize discussion, and improve decision-making time. Board time is precious. It should not be wasted on reporting that can be done through pre-reads and ancillary conversations. Deliver the board book far enough in advance, so participants can read it, consider it, and prepare questions.

Maintain an annual cycle of evergreen topics. Certain subjects need to be addressed every year, and it is beneficial to spread them out over twelve months to make meetings more manageable. Examples include strategy development, budgets, succession planning, performance evaluations, compensation, and risk management.

Make time for self-evaluation. Effective agendas reserve time for the board to evaluate itself. Board evaluations are complex and essential to board performance; it's important to include this time on the agenda at least annually.

7

Role Of Committees: Audit, Compensation, And Nominating

Committees are easy targets for pundits and jokesters. Consider these jests:

"If Columbus had an advisory committee, he would probably still be at the dock."—Arthur Goldberg

"A committee is a group of people who individually can do nothing but who, as a group, can meet and decide that nothing can be done."—Fred Allen

"A committee is a group that keeps minutes and loses hours." —Milton Berle

Humor aside, this chapter is not to belittle committees but to point out how important they are to proper company governance.

The three board committees that are most often found are audit, compensation, and nominating.

Audit is usually first and happens when the bank requires an audit, which someone other than management needs to oversee. Compensation is next since pay is always an issue. Nominating is last since the board needs to sustain itself.

Let's examine the three committees and the role of each.

An Owner's View Of The Audit Committee

Private companies typically do not audit their books unless an outside party requires it. Audits are a material expense and require great effort.

The bank is typically the first party to require an audit. Outside investors are usually next to ask for one, either before investing or as a condition of their investment. Having worked with almost one hundred private companies, I can't recall a single case of a company choosing to be audited if not required to do so.

The first audit can be quite difficult if the company's accounting practices are not consistent with Generally Acceptable Accounting Principles (GAAP). This is often the most grueling part of professionalizing the accounting function of a private company.

A first-year audit may be a balance sheet only audit since the accountant will need to audit the beginning balance sheet of the previous year to opine on the income statement. When given a choice, consider doing a balance sheet only audit for the first year and then the entire statement the second year. The second and third years tend to run smoother.

A private company without a functioning board can conduct an audit without having an audit committee. Companies form boards to help ownership and management deal with increasing size, complexity, and risk. The audit committee is typically the first subcommittee to be formed.

The audit committee is responsible for making sure the financial statements are understandable and reliable, internal controls are effective, and policies on ethics and fraud are understood and enforced. It also oversees litigation and regulatory matters and selects and manages the relationship with the public accounting firm and communications with any internal auditors on staff.

If you are forming your first audit committee, what are the key issues to think about from an ownership perspective? Here are the key questions I recommend my clients consider:

Who is the audience for the audit?

Most private companies do not follow GAAP accounting. One benefit of being private is that you can craft your statements to enhance decision-making. But variations from GAAP will need to be negotiated with the auditors. These discussions will be a balance between accounting inertia, management preferences, and the auditor's requirements. The goal is to get a clean opinion.

If you are doing an audit, you are doing it for a reason. Who is asking for it and what are their needs? While it doesn't change the audit process, knowing your audience will help in resolving the open issues.

Do you have an "unqualified opinion," also known as a clean opinion?

An audit includes several documents: the audited financial statement, the auditor's opinion letter to the audit committee, and a management representation letter. Each piece needs to be examined by the committee. Once the numbers are confirmed, understanding the letters and how to interpret them is where the committee needs to lean in. The goal is to have a clean opinion from the auditor.

A clean opinion means the audit team believes the financial statements are reasonably stated, i.e., free of material misstatement. Audits are not designed to detect fraud and do not detect fraud in most cases.

Anything other than a clean opinion needs to be investigated and weighed. Auditors are typically cautious and specific in their wording so a slight change in wording needs attention.

Did management cooperate?

Audit committees are the critical element in the governance system that keeps management accountable. Otherwise, there could be no real oversight over the executive team.

In most private companies, there are only a few people who work directly with the auditors. The people running the business are usually the same as the people who own the business.

A key function of the audit committee is to work with the outside auditor to assess if management is cooperative with the audit process. It may seem odd for the auditor to report back to the people they investigated but that is how it works. Having outsiders on the audit committee is a good way to protect investors. If you are a sizable owner who is not active in the business, you may want to be on the audit committee, as that is the best way to protect your investment.

Are there any exceptions of consequence?

Are there reasons to be concerned with how the numbers are put together? Were there any surprises? Were they material? Remember the auditor's opinion means the statements are materially correct, not that the auditor will catch every error. Understanding the definition of what the auditor considers material is crucial to understanding the audit.

The audit committee must get a list of proposed adjustment and adjustments that were considered but not made. If the amount of a single account is off, or the total of the financial statements are off without an adjustment, that adjustment needs to be understood.

Once the issues are understood, the committee needs to apply judgment to resolve differences and attempt to move to a clean opinion.

Did you remember the executive session?

Once the audit process is completed, there should be an executive session to discuss any possible concerns the auditors may have had with the management team. Was the CFO uncooperative? Was there any suspicious activity? What can we do better?

This is the time for the committee to probe, ask tough questions, and listen closely to both what is said, and more importantly, what might not be said. This is the time for outsiders to step up since they are often more able to ask uncomfortable questions than insiders.

In long-term relationships, the executive session tends to be perfunctory since everyone knows each other, and the audit process does not vary much year to year. That is a sign of success.

A great audit process has no surprises; it just needs to get done. But it should give owners comfort that their assets are being managed properly and appropriate safeguards are in place.

Getting Started: Private Company Compensation Committees[10]

While the work of public company compensation committees is well understood and receives considerable investor attention, the same cannot be said for private company compensation committees. Most private company boards don't use standing subcommittees, so the owners lack the point of view of public company directors experienced in this type of work.

For most private companies, setting executive compensation is an annual exercise that is less than optimized. Whether it is due to economic constraints or personal friendships, some important discussions just don't happen often enough, if at all. If a private company board intends to start a formal compensation committee, here are some important questions to consider:

How do the base pay, annual bonus, and long-term incentives align with the company's strategic plan and market realities? Most private companies have well-established routines for addressing compensation. Since leadership tends to be stable, the decision-making behaviors and unspoken metrics are known.

During economic booms, compensation discussions tend to revolve around the question, "Are we at risk of losing executives?"

During moderate times, the question leans toward, "Is the pay fair for what the executives are doing?"

In a downturn, the thinking is more, "How can we afford to compensate executives?"

Performance reviews at private companies are often summaries, not data-rich exercises. They are also likely to be siloed and not viewed in terms of the overarching goals of the organization.

My experience suggests the board can improve these areas by asking the following questions:

1. How has the individual's performance driven success to achieve strategic goals?
2. Is the individual a good fit for the role they are in both today and in the future?

3. How does the individual exemplify the values and culture we aspire to demonstrate?

Looking at this triad of criteria sets the stage for a better evaluation of how impactful the organization's leaders are in achieving ownership objectives, and therefore how to compensate them for their impact.

Does the company have the right data for benchmarking? Most private companies have access to limited compensation data. Their trade associations often provide compensation data specific to their industry, but I have found such reports to have limitations. They are indicative but not sufficiently informative. Often, there is not enough data to have confidence in what the numbers are saying.

When you ask about location adjustments or niche adjustments, there isn't sufficient information, and you need to interpolate to form an opinion. Public companies have an advantage in that their data is rich and plentiful in comparison.

Private companies may be reluctant to pay for something that is often seen as not having enough utility ("but we only use it once a year"), hindering access to higher-quality data insights. There are many high-quality compensation consultants who can help, but they are a greater expense than the data. So owners do without it—at the expense of more appropriate and competitive executive compensation.

How does the company deal with underperformers that can't be easily replaced? Private companies tend to have smaller and less well-developed management teams than public companies do. Executive turnover tends to be lower for many reasons. Personal loyalty and relationships tend to be stronger since there is no public market pressure for performance.

If a senior executive isn't cutting it but is not easily replaced, how much risk do you want to take in transitioning to a new player? What is the value of "the devil you know" versus going to the open market? While there is value in organizational stability, what is the cost of condoning unacceptable performance? If the problem includes objectionable behaviors, the cost could be more than you think. These types of concerns often prevent needed change.

How much should the company let loyalty overrule merit? As the saying goes, if you are making money, the bank is happy, and if you are paying your taxes, you can do what you want at a private company. If the management team has been together for a long time, personal friendships can get in the way of evaluating and acting upon poor performance. How are you going to balance these conflicts?

Instances of executive underperformance and excessive loyalty are typically well-known throughout the ranks of the business. A decision to accept these shortcomings tells the staff what the real culture is, what gets rewarded, and what negative behaviors are tolerated—at least for the lucky few.

How aggressively should the company set goals? Maybe more critically, should there be any leniency if the company doesn't make the goals? For a private company, if the owners are happy with the business results, then they are good enough. If there is no outside pressure, there tends to be incentive to reward people even when they don't reach their goals (the "let's be nice" syndrome).

This is where outside directors can help the owners and managers balance conflicts. The outsiders should not have these biases and know they have been engaged to provide clear-eyed perspectives on what is best for the business. The outsider directors, and the board as a whole, need to serve as a compass through these difficult decisions.

Performance and compensation are issues in every organization. As the business grows, the issues become more complicated, and the risks of talent flight increase. While much of the work of a compensation committee is formulaic, the bigger issues require deeper consideration. The hardest part of this work is often the judgment to balance facts and figures against emotion, relationships, and the risks and rewards that are not measured in dollars and cents.

These are the quandaries that allow board members to earn their keep.

With this in mind, how does the business owner keep board members fully engaged? Let's look at the ways to keep board work fresh, including the role of the nominating committee.

Ways Owners Can Keep Their Boards Fresh

From time to time, I hear concerns from owners about their board's effectiveness, and sometimes, about specific members. Like all human organizations, boards need to be attended to so they are healthy and well-functioning.

When trying to help owners evaluate their concerns, I suggest they look through two lenses: First, what type of board is it? Second, how mature is it?

There are four types of boards in private companies: consulting boards, junior advisory boards, full advisory boards, and fiduciary boards. Venture capital or private equity-backed firms and ESOPs will have fiduciary boards which, to varying degrees, fall outside of these comments.

Consulting boards will meet one or two days per year, usually when there is a pressing issue. They tend to be narrowly focused on a few issues. They are sometimes seen as an evolution from a CEO peer group, such as Vistage or YPO, and are usually preferred by smaller businesses.

Junior advisory boards have the formal structures of a full board but focus only on a subset of issues. Strategy and cash flow are the typical subjects. Executive compensation and succession planning are typically off limits.

Full advisory boards are similar to fiduciary boards but without the vote. While similar, the full advisory boards still tend to not have the same mandate as a fiduciary board. Outsiders are usually engaged in succession planning, management compensation, and management performance evaluation. It just depends on how sophisticated the ownership group is, and where they want help from outsiders.

Boards mature over time, just like people. For years zero to two, or close to that, boards are like children finding their way in the world.

It often takes a full year (one cycle) for a new board to find a rhythm. It will take longer for the outsiders to build effective relationships. They don't spend much time together and need enough common problem-solving to gel. Obviously, a crisis helps—throw them in the fire together.

The members need to figure out how to work with each other, deal with conflict, understand the company culture, and draw conclusions on what is in bounds versus out of bounds for them.

The next phase, years two to five, is like being a teenager. You know what to do, you know what is expected, and you are striving to be an adult but you may need more time to get there. This analogy specifically excludes the undesirable aspects of teenager behavior.

Maturity is what happens thereafter. If the participants don't change, things tend to be stable. Business conditions will drive the issues and changes that the board wrestles with. This last phase is when owners and chairs need to focus on board evaluations, term limits, and how to keep the board fresh.

So who is driving this discussion? If there is a well-developed nominating committee, it should be leading the discussion. But many private company boards do not have committees, and the chair is the owner who is not skilled in this area. The outside directors are not going to push this issue until the problem is unavoidable. Some will vote with their feet.

Since all governance issues go to the primary shareholder, here is my advice for them to consider:

Reassess near-term challenges. What issues does the board need to address over the next three to five years? Are the current members well-suited to those challenges? They may have been the right people for the past problems, but new problems suggest new talent is needed.

Evaluate and refine your expectations. Do you know what you want your board to accomplish? Have you provided a clear mandate to the individuals so they know what is expected of each of them? Is it an expectations issue or a communications issue that is causing discomfort or underachievement?

Be sure to understand the outsiders' expectations. Some owners underutilize their outside directors. The outsiders actively decide how much time to spend on board work. They will tend to lean in when things are interesting or when they see they can make an impact.

The most powerful thing an owner can do to get more from their outsiders is to ask for their attention. "Hey, this is important, can you take a look and tell me what you think?" Outsiders are cautious not to step on toes, and thus wait to be invited into some subjects. There is a fine balance with regard to these inquiries that also needs consideration to avoid overreach.

Ask your professionals to weigh in. It is likely that your attorneys, accountants, auditors, and consultants interact with the board. It is reasonable to get their impressions of how the board operates. They usually know the company well and have an opinion but will not share thoughts if not asked.

Measure impact and take action if needed. Feedback is the breakfast of champions. Board evaluations are a key means to keep a board healthy and vital. There are many ways to do this; you just need to find one that works for you. Look for the silent signals of a poor fit: missing meetings, being unprepared, poor body language, and a lack of insightful questioning. If the data suggests there is an issue, don't let it fester.

Don't be afraid to mix it up. Sometimes a little change to mix things up is good. Guest members are common in this regard, or a change of location or meeting structure. A new agenda pattern to stimulate ideas may be needed. Keep things fresh to drive engagement.

Boards are a powerful tool for creating value for owners and reducing the risks of ownership. But learning how to use them requires time and attention. Good owners understand this and invest the time to get more from their boards.

Warning: Do not put this off until "someday." As science writer Timothy Ferris put it, "'Someday' is a disease that will take your dreams to the grave with you."

While committees often do the heavy lifting within a governance structure, it is the board as a whole that is responsible for oversight.

What's Next

The next chapter will demonstrate how a healthy oversight function operates.

Chapter 7 Takeaways

Role Of Committees: Audit, Compensation, and Nominating

Know that boards mature over time. The need for and effectiveness of committees will evolve as the board matures.

Be aware that a great audit process has no surprises. An audit needs to be done. But it should give owners comfort that their assets are being managed properly and appropriate safeguards are in place.

Conduct management performance reviews. My experience suggests boards can improve performance reviews by asking these questions: How has the individual's performance driven success to achieve strategic goals? Is the individual a good fit for the role they are in, both today and in the future? How does the individual exemplify the values and culture we aspire to demonstrate?

Use boards to reduce risk. Boards are a powerful tool for creating value for owners and reducing the risks of ownership. But learning how to use them requires time and attention. Good owners understand this and invest the time to get more from their boards.

Keep your board fresh. Many private company boards do not have committees, and the chair is the owner, who is not skilled in this area. The lack of a nominating committee may cause the board to become stale. The outside directors are not going to push this issue until it is unavoidable.

Reassess near-term challenges. What issues does the board need to address over the next three to five years? Are the current members well-suited to those challenges? They may have been the right people for the past problems but new problems suggest new talent is needed.

Evaluate and refine your expectations. Do you know what you want your board to accomplish? Is it an expectations issue or a communications issue that is causing discomfort or underachievement?

8

Board Function: Oversight

Consider the wise words of Pearl Zhu, a global corporate executive, author, and digital business visionary. Here is her take on boards: "'Group thinking,' or lack of courage to ask the tough and strategic questions, is the chief weakness of boards today."[11]

According to Zhu, the role of a functioning board "is to pull management out of the trees to see the forest."

However, most private companies do not have functioning boards capable of letting the business leaders see the forest from the trees. In a word: oversight.

Developing Effective Board Oversight For A Private Company

When you research what corporate boards do, oversight is typically the first item on the list. But what does "oversight" mean? Surprisingly, while oversight may be the most important role of a corporate board, it has a loose or open-ended definition. Public companies will give terse definitions of their board's oversight role, but these typically don't translate well into the private world.

The best definition I have heard is the old phrase of "noses in, fingers out." The first part refers to what a good director is: a cop on a beat, looking for trouble but not making any. "Fingers out" is an admonition that directors should not cross the line to interfere with management's responsibilities.

A newer version of this saying is "noses in, fingers out, sensors on." The addition of "sensors on" means to have capabilities to anticipate issues before they become actual problems. Easier to say than do, but it is an attitude every director can adapt readily.

The spectrum of private companies includes VC- and PE-owned portfolio companies and ESOPs in addition to traditional private and family businesses. The former three ownership types tend to be more like public companies; these notes are focused on private and family-owned businesses.

Outside directors at a private business can be anywhere on the spectrum of overactive to totally passive. This often depends on the board's mandate from its owners. Do the outsiders feel empowered to push and probe?

While less applicable to fiduciary boards, there is a great variation among advisory boards. My observations are that there are three types of advisory boards: consulting, junior, and full advisory boards.

The type of advisory board is typically inverse to the degree of inquiry granted to the outsiders. Typically, the more authority given to the outsiders, the more likely they are to exercise discretion regarding oversight. For example, if the outsiders are not involved in executive compensation, or issues within the ownership group, they will be disinclined to probe deeply on sensitive issues.

There are also industry variations on oversight. Businesses that are heavily regulated (e.g., financial, trucking) are used to extra scrutiny. Private widget companies, especially if they have no bank or outside investors, often get skittish at the basic questions.

With that as background, here is my basic list of oversight questions that every outside advisor or director should be considering.

Trouble With A Capital T

Trouble comes in many forms, but it usually ties back to how assets are managed and how people behave. Sometimes there are external factors that may be overlooked, e.g., a change in regulations that is missed. Other times there are just bad actors causing trouble.

Here is a punch list of topics, and the questions to ask to get the lay of the land:

Financial. If there is no audit, are there checks and balances in recording entries? Are there formal cash controls? Are there two people reviewing actions before cash leaves the bank? Is there a written Levels of Authority document stipulating how oversight escalates as disbursements increase in size or nature? Where could a malicious actor cause a problem?

Regulatory. Do we know all of our regulatory requirements, and are we in compliance? While OSHA and EEOC are the dominant forces here, many industries have their own regulators that need to be satisfied. How seriously does management take these responsibilities?

Human Resources. Do we have an HR manual, and do we follow our own policies? Are the policies current with today's market conditions? Is there a way for employees to safely complain and get resolutions? If not, their frustration is more likely to become a lawsuit or adverse regulatory filing.

Ethical Issues. While often the most difficult to deal with, ethical challenges often pose the greatest risk, as they are binary. Employees will compare your mission/vision/values statements to your actions and will vote on how you handled it.

Technology. While this includes cybersecurity, the topic is broader. Businesses are a collection of people, products, and processes. Business processes are executed through the technology infrastructure. As businesses grow and change, their legacy systems tend to lag behind the business's needs. Knowing where and when to make major upgrades versus patches is important, since you change how the business functions.

Legal. Lawsuits are almost unavoidable in our society. They need to be managed as business matters; who was wrong tends to fall aside at some point. Is management on top of this? Is it managed as a business function or just a side activity disproportionate to the risk?

Insurance. Are all the insurable risks reviewed annually? Are the coverages up to date? Are the carriers appropriate for the situation? Are the agents providing the level of service needed by the business?

Customer Requirements. In some businesses, arrangements with customers require overview to protect future revenues. Beyond price, quality, and delivery, what else goes into the relationship that is a risk to the business? Are our salespeople properly matched to the customer's culture? Does the customer have expectations, e.g., directed charitable giving, that need to be addressed?

This is not an exhaustive list but a starting point. A well-designed onboarding process will provide this information to new directors and then be updated annually for the full board to understand. Many companies have unique functions that will add to this list.

The culture and management personalities will have a heavy influence on how oversight is performed.

Oversight is an open-ended subject at the board level. It truly exercises the definition of judgment for individual advisors and directors.

The unknown isn't what it used to be. We live in an increasingly volatile and complex world, and board members who can manage increased complexity are needed.

Managing Increasing Complexity In A Growing Business

Most owners know the difference between working on their business versus working in their business. As businesses grow, they get harder to manage because they become more complicated. This complexity creates that ever-increasing sense of inertia that prevents you from growing as fast as you think you should. I believe anticipating, identifying, and resolving complexity is what is needed to facilitate scalability.

There is no easy way to measure complexity or an increase in complexity. The most likely signs of change are step functions that create span of control, capital, and operational challenges. Most people can get an initial benchmark of complexity just by knowing the revenue range or headcount. But revenue range has very different meanings for different types of companies. Think about software versus manufacturing versus retail businesses.

If you are an outsider looking in, these questions should provide context to understand what the owners are facing.

What is the depth and breadth of the management team? Do the founders still do everything, or are their senior functional leaders empowered to make decisions? Have the founders learned how to achieve results through people and not just by driving performance through themselves? Does the management team have enough qualified leaders so each pillar of scalability has a driver?

Do they engage many consultants? It is usually true that you should rent skills you don't need to own, but having too many consultants suggests a lack of native capabilities. Managing those outsiders can be a distraction as well.

What decisions are delegated down versus tightly controlled at the top? Most private companies do not have a written policy on spending limits or hiring and firing staff. The culture dictates these rules, so you tend to know without being asked or told. Scalability requires everyone to know their limits of authority and know how to get decisions made with full buy-in.

How many industry verticals, geographies, or SKUs does the company have? Each of these metrics adds a notch to complexity. A company could choose to be narrowly focused for a variety of reasons, but niche players tend to see limited growth.

How complicated is the capital structure? Is there equity from sources other than friends and family? Is the bank loan secured or based on cash flow only? Are there multiple lenders or investors involved? The ability to execute these transactions indicates increasing levels of financial competence, which is needed to fund a greater degree of scalability.

What business systems are they using? Software vendors design their platforms for specific needs. Many are based on the industry they serve. Virtually all will have a targeted client size. This may be measured in headcount, ledger accounts, or transaction volume. These are ways for vendors to measure the client's complexity to see if their platform is a good fit. It also indicates what management is planning to do with the business.

Identifying Complexity

Those are the questions an outsider might ask to quickly understand the state of the business. But what is the discussion inside the boardroom? How does the company assess itself? If you are the owner or part of management, these are the questions and issues likely to be on your mind.

Do we need a CFO? Companies start with a bookkeeper, then move toward a comptroller to make sure debits equal credits and add some reporting capabilities. A CFO is usually focused on the capital structure and financial analysis and often takes on IT and HR if no one else can handle those functions.

Do we need to talk about bringing on a senior HR or IT leader? Similar to bringing on a CFO, these are in other functional departments and require close consideration.

Do we need to look at a bigger ERP or CRM system? Large IT systems are expensive and may be difficult to transition to; companies often migrate when they can no longer avoid them. If you find yourself frequently discussing workaround solutions or using spreadsheets to cover IT gaps, that is a warning signal.

Do I need of board of advisors, as my friends suggest? This discussion usually starts when a company is around $25 million to $30 million in revenue and becomes more common as the company grows. Boards add value by providing outside experience, perspective, and judgment to help companies move forward.

Scalability and Complexity

So now that you have the tools to recognize the signs of increasing complexity, what can you do to increase your scalability and grow your business?

Recognize the forces at play. It is hard to address issues if you don't acknowledge and understand them. If you answer the questions above and feel good about your situation, keep driving forward. If not, you have decisions to make.

Understand your ability to manage change. Change is hard. How adaptable is your organization? What might you need to do to get your staff ready for what is ahead of them? Modifying your culture is harder than hiring a CFO or installing an ERP. Remember, change starts at the top. You likely need to demonstrate the desired change of behavior yourself to convince your staff that they need to change, also.

Set priorities on how much change you can handle at once. What needs to happen serially, e.g., IT system selection, migration, training, then impact, versus what can happen in parallel such as recruiting a CFO and CHRO at the same time? Assessing how much change the organization can handle in short periods of time is a key choice to make.

Assess if outside help improves the change process. Consultants and interim executives can serve a useful role in transitioning an organization. Consider using them as a bridge to where you need to get to. You likely don't need them forever.

Assessing complexity and managing change can be hard, so it is important to stay focused on where you want to get to. Effective business leaders always plan for the future.

Boards Should Anticipate Future Problems

To quote the late motivational speaker and author Zig Ziglar: "The media has successfully predicted ten of the last three recessions."

But for boards I prefer this other view from Ziglar: "Expect the best. Prepare for the worst. Capitalize on what comes."

Great partnerships are based on aligned interests and accepted rules for managing conflict. The bylaws or operating agreement of an entity codify how the most important decisions get made and who gets to make them. The best relationships do not require the bylaws to resolve ownership conflicts in the future.

The root cause of conflict among business owners is typically a failure to anticipate problems and negotiate resolution mechanisms before the trouble starts. Often, one party doesn't want to "send the wrong signal" at the start of the relationship. The excitement of a new venture or bringing on a capital partner often pushes aside the need to negotiate these types of details.

Keep Bylaws And Founding Documents Current

Getting it right at the beginning is the best way to manage relationships between partners. But needs change over time, whether driven by market conditions, new opportunities, ownership changes, or chance. That is why it is important to review your bylaws or operating agreements every three to five years to make sure they are current with your situation. These documents should be reviewed well in advance of a capital event.

Unless you own 100 percent of the business yourself, you need to play chess, not checkers. If you do own 100 percent of the equity, you need to decide what happens when you are not able to be decisive.

Your goal is to have current documents that anticipate future challenges; don't wait until you have a problem, e.g., death, disability, termination, or liquidity event, to decide the rules.

The most common need is to have a buyback clause or put/call arrangement in the founding documents. After all, you agreed to be in business with your partner but not your deceased partner's spouse.

In a family business, ownership succession is typically the biggest risk to that business's continuity.

The Board's Role In Business Ownership Conflicts

As previously noted, boards are responsible for strategy, oversight, capital structure, management continuity, and risk management. The board should not necessarily be involved in ownership succession since that is the realm of the owner, not the board. But effective boards become responsible to assure that someone competent is in charge of ownership succession. It is in the best interest of the organization.

So if you are an outside director in this situation, what should you do if you see the ownership group is not addressing its own continuity?

Dealing With Ownership Conflicts

As with most matters in the boardroom, it depends. But here are the questions to ask yourself once you become concerned:

How do you fulfill your fiduciary duty? As a director, you are bound by the duties of care and loyalty. This situation is a test of both. You may want to consult the firm's counsel or perhaps an outside counsel to make sure you fully understand the legal ramifications of the situation.

What are the group dynamics? In other words, who is on which side? A person's affiliation with a particular faction will influence their decisions and behaviors. Delicate situations like a business ownership conflict, when people play for "all the marbles," tend to bring out undesirable behaviors that need to be managed to achieve a resolution.

Who can actually help solve the problem? This is often construed as "who can I trust to work on the issues?" If you have been in the boardroom for a few years, you should already have a good read on people's EQ as well as their IQ, and how those forces will influence the situation.

What if there is no one in the ownership group competent to make a decision? With successive generations, there tends to be decreasing interest or competence to manage a family business. It is perfectly normal to have non-family members running a family-owned business, but someone still needs to represent ownership. If the fiduciary board has little guidance from the family, this becomes a true test of fiduciary duty. In that case, there is even more reason to get an unbiased third-party opinion of how to deal with conflict.

Who will communicate with staff, customers, and suppliers to assure continuity? Staff, customers, and suppliers may not be involved in what's going on, but they are keenly interested in it since it likely affects their livelihood. Think about it: the ownership problem may determine whether or not they have a paycheck, and all they can do is sit on the sidelines and hope someone tells them about the situation. As a director, you want these people to stay focused on their business mission and not look for another source of income.

How do you keep it out of the courts and out of the media? Good common sense suggests you want to keep business owner conflicts out of the court—and out of the press. Those forums will only make the situation more complicated and less pleasant. Not everyone has aligned interests on this point.

Outside Directors Can Step In When No One Else Can

Typically, the outside professionals become the catalyst for change when there is no decision-maker. Their goal is to protect their clients, which initiates action. The independent director needs to understand their motivations and possible conflicts of interest, and from there discuss a sensible course of action with their colleagues.

How Boards Navigate Crises

One of a board's most valuable functions is navigating crises. Different voices and opinions naturally have a stabilizing effect. They yield more rational thought and reduce panic. They also bring a diversity of knowledge, experiences, and resources to the table. Since crises like COVID-19 often affect management personally, boards are responsible for preventing emotion from clouding sound business judgment.

As management focuses on handling short-term logistical adaptations to issues such as social distancing regulations and supply chain disruptions, boards should be able to keep the business's long-term mission in sight. A board should be able to preserve a business's competitive advantage through digital transformation and customer experience initiatives while monitoring industry competition—even as management is still busy putting out fires.

Having a diverse board with at least one member who has crisis management experience is vital. Though COVID-19 resists comparison to past catastrophes in many ways, members who have navigated events such as 9/11 and the

2008 financial crisis have experience overcoming uncertainty that is valuable during any distressing event.

Your board members should have accumulated enough battle scars to say, "Here's what we have learned in the past. Here's what you need to think about now and into the future." At the end of the day, you want your company's board to be filled with people you know will be able to handle the unknown because they've done it before.

What's Next

I hope you rarely will be in crisis mode with the barbarians at the gate. Instead of defending the empire, board members should be strategic catalysts to expand the empire. In the following chapter let's explore the board's role in developing and executing strategy.

Chapter 8 Takeaways

Board Function: Oversight

Understand what board oversight is. The phrase "noses in, fingers out, sensors on" describes the mindset of a good director.

Understand complexity. There is no easy way to measure complexity or an increase in complexity. The most likely signs of change are step functions that create span of control, capital, and operational challenges.

Focus on scalability and complexity. Understand your ability to manage change. Change is hard. How adaptable is your organization? What might you need to do to get your staff ready for what is ahead of them?

Know that boards should anticipate future problems. Great partnerships are based on aligned interests and accepted rules for managing conflict. The bylaws or operating agreement of an entity codify how the most important decisions get made and who gets to make them.

Keep your organizational documents current. You should review your bylaws or operating agreement every three to five years to make sure they are current with your situation. These documents should be reviewed well in advance of a capital event.

Realize that boards reduce risks. Your board members should have accumulated enough battle scars to say, "Here's what we have learned in the past. Here's what you need to think about now and into the future." At the end of the day, you want your company's board to be filled with people you know will be able to handle the unknown because they've done it before.

9

Board Function: Strategy Development And Execution

Jim Rohn was a renowned author, entrepreneur, Hall of Fame speaker, and business strategist. He once said, "Success is 20 percent skills and 80 percent strategy. You might know how to succeed but more importantly, what's your plan to succeed?"

Successful strategy is done top down; implementation is done bottom up.

You build a business strategy from the top, working down, layer by layer. You keep peeling back until you have it figured out—and then it's time to act, implementing the plan from the bottom up. It is a virtuous loop if done properly.

If you have the right plan and execute the details properly, you should get the right results. Lots of companies have great ideas but if they can't execute, it doesn't matter.

Understanding Your Competitive Model

Strategy was once defined as trying to gain an unfair advantage in the marketplace. Michael Porter published a book in 1980 that reframed the discussion on competitive strategy.[12] Businesses compete to produce superior returns for the investors. These returns depend on the industry and how a business positions itself within that industry.

Every industry has a natural growth rate, e.g., software versus grocery, and a natural level of profitability, e.g., luxury items versus commodity items. Once you pick your industry, the rules of competition are pretty much set. But you can control how you position your business within that industry via strategy.

Porter defined five forces in strategy development:

- Rivalry among competitors
- Bargaining power of customers
- Threats from new entrants
- Threats from substitute products/services
- Bargaining power of suppliers

Your ability to gain an unfair advantage depends on understanding these five forces and making decisions to do better than your competition overall within your market.

Porter's Model Of Competition

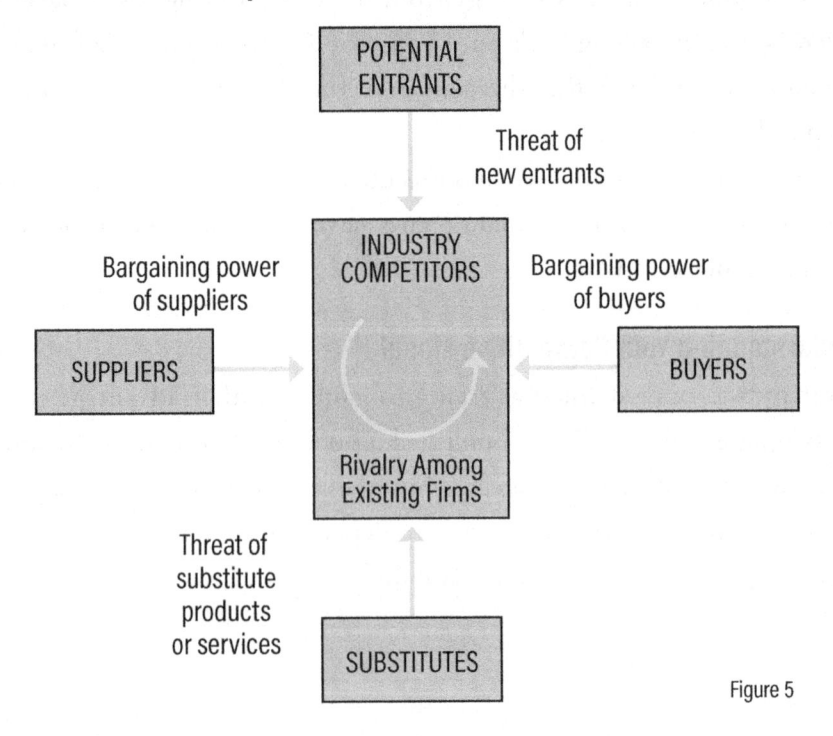

Figure 5

Porter's Definition Of The Five Basic Competitive Strategies

STRATEGIC ADVANTAGE

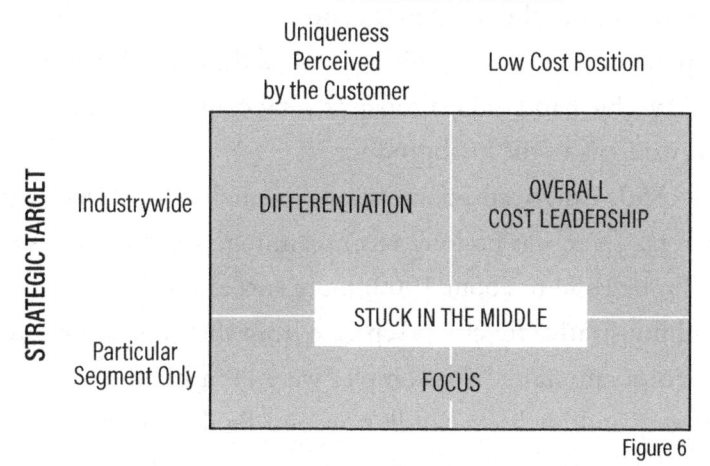

	Uniqueness Perceived by the Customer	Low Cost Position
Industrywide	DIFFERENTIATION	OVERALL COST LEADERSHIP
	STUCK IN THE MIDDLE	
Particular Segment Only	FOCUS	

STRATEGIC TARGET

Figure 6

What you don't want to be is "stuck in the middle." That means you are roadkill waiting to happen since you have no advantage over your competition. You need to have a sustainable long-term competitive advantage if your business is to survive and prosper.

From this work, the phrase "value proposition" became popular. But what does this phrase mean? Simply put: Know who your customers are, deeply understand their needs, and price your offering where your customers consider it to be at least fair value to them. This process will force you to think about how to grow your business and increase your profitability.

Structure Follows Strategy

Once you have developed a competitive strategy based on your industry that provides you with a long-term competitive advantage, how do you organize your business to execute that strategy?

The seminal work on industrial organization was written by Alfred Chandler in 1962.[13] He was the first to tie together business strategy, organizational structure, market dynamics, and entrepreneurship. His famous quote is "Structure follows strategy," meaning the organization's structure depends on its business strategy.

Chandler's research focused on American industry from 1850 to about 1920. This research categorized businesses and their evolution. He defined four stages of industrial development and provided specific case studies to prove his points. While Adam Smith described the invisible hand, Chandler defined the visible hand as "a company's total control of the entire process from raw materials to the final product."

Until 1850, American businesses were small enterprises focused on local markets. There was no long-term planning, and the owners were the business. From 1850 to about 1900, more successful businesses started to develop administrative functions separate from their operations. Today we call them corporate staff. Two examples were John Jacob Astor's American Fur Company and Nicholas Biddle's Second Bank. But the Erie Railroad set the benchmark since its expansion required forward planning on a scale not yet seen in business.

Moving into the 1900s, the new century presented opportunities for vertical integration as demonstrated by Gustavus Swift (meatpacking) and Singer sewing machines. Later in this phase, horizontal expansion was exhibited by the trusts and federations of the early 1900s. National Biscuit is cited as an example.

In the early twentieth century, these businesses had become moribund so their structures evolved again. Multidivisional, decentralized structures were developed to make large, complex organizations more manageable. Moving to and through World War II, with the American economy growing to be the largest in the world, the old ways of doing things no longer worked. The four examples presented were DuPont (product focus), GM (divisional boundaries based on market strategy), Standard Oil (multi-departmental structure), and Sears (multidivisional organization).

This research is from the last century before any form of modern technology existed. Are these theories still relevant? Yes. The globalization and supply chain issues of the last fifty years have forced businesses to reorganize yet again. Compartmentalized, just-in-time supply chains have replaced vertical integration. Look at how many logistics firms now exist. Look at the scale of FedEx, UPS, and DHL. Business systems have moved from timeshare to big iron, to desktops, to client/server, to the cloud.

Since COVID-19, the globalization trend has reversed to increase reshoring, or onshoring as it may be called, to reduce domestic business risks. In each iteration, businesses have reorganized production planning, logistics, inventory management, customer service, and administrative functions.

As businesses decide what functions they need to own versus outsource to be competitive, they have reorganized. Structure still follows strategy.

When you think about how you compete, is your business organized to deploy your strategy most effectively? If not, how should you reorganize your business?

Converting Theory Into Practice For Your Business

While reviewing the work of Chandler and Porter is necessary to understand the big picture of competition, private company owners live in the "real world," so let's bring this down to what you live with every day.

You must get the strategy right first but that is not enough. You then need to execute fearlessly and be ruthlessly loyal to the strategy. This chart sums up what I see in the marketplace:

Sustained Success Requires Both Strategy and Execution

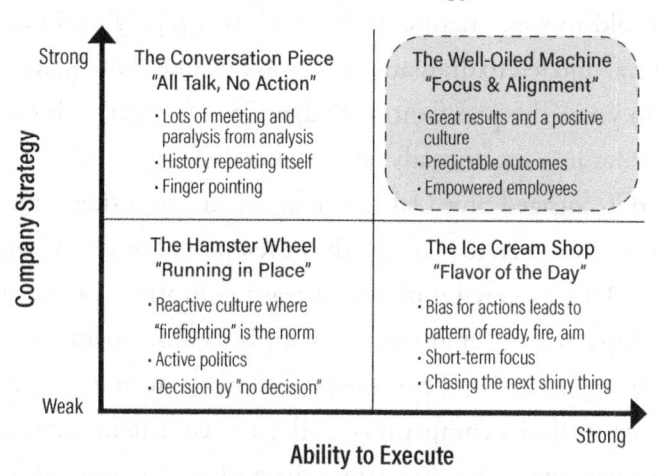

	Ability to Execute – Weak	Ability to Execute – Strong
Company Strategy – Strong	**The Conversation Piece** "All Talk, No Action" • Lots of meeting and paralysis from analysis • History repeating itself • Finger pointing	**The Well-Oiled Machine** "Focus & Alignment" • Great results and a positive culture • Predictable outcomes • Empowered employees
Company Strategy – Weak	**The Hamster Wheel** "Running in Place" • Reactive culture where "firefighting" is the norm • Active politics • Decision by "no decision"	**The Ice Cream Shop** "Flavor of the Day" • Bias for actions leads to pattern of ready, fire, aim • Short-term focus • Chasing the next shiny thing

(Graphic courtesy of Blue Oak Strategy, used with permission)

Figure 7

So how do you become a well-oiled machine? By thinking hard about your mission, vision, and key imperatives.

Mission is, "Who are we?"

Vision is, "Where are we going?"

Key imperatives show, "How are we going to get there?"

Figuring this out is what all companies need to do to be successful. But for most private companies, getting this right is difficult due to having fewer resources than larger public companies.

This case study, BadgerCo, was prepared by Tim McClure at Blue Oak Strategy (https://www.blueoakstrategy.com/).

It is an effective toolset for private companies to organize these thoughts and convert them into a specific, measurable, and meaningful action plan. While most owners work on mission, vision, and key imperatives, few have the time and focus on pulling it together succinctly, as presented here.

Case Study: Path To Consistent, Profitable Growth

BadgerCo is a custom fabricator of industrial process equipment. The company provides made-to-order modular systems mounted on skids or trailers to remote operating locations. BadgerCo had grown to $13 million in annual sales driven almost entirely by one large account (an OEM in the power generation industry). The revenue cycle was long, and while the custom "build to spec" nature of the work was highly profitable, projects were "lumpy" and led to dramatic swings in revenue from quarter to quarter and year to year. The president of BadgerCo was eager to break this cycle and grow sales in a more steady and predictable way.

BadgerCo engaged Blue Oak, a management consulting firm specializing in research and strategy, to facilitate the development of a multi-year strategic plan. Blue Oak chartered a planning team comprised of executives from each key department: engineering, supply chain, operations, sales and finance. Through a series of planning sessions, the team reviewed company performance, analyzed competitors, and gathered data for key end-markets. They identified the company's strengths and weaknesses, took inventory of competitive assets, and prioritized opportunities for improvement and growth. Together, the BadgerCo leadership team painted a clear picture of the company they wanted to become with a roadmap to make it happen.

There are many ways to approach strategic planning and capture the output of the process. Blue Oak utilized a Strategic Framework model to organize and communicate strategic goals and decisions. The Strategic Framework is structured like a book with three chapters. Each chapter answers a fundamental question: Who are we? Where are we going? How are we going to get there? The contents of each chapter vary based on the needs of the business. The critical, must-have components are: Mission, Vision, Key Imperatives (focus area over the life of the vision) and Key Initiatives (annual initiatives, projects, and "work to do" under each imperative). A summary of BadgerCo's strategic plan is shown below.

Having the leadership team aligned around this game plan was a breakthrough, but the plan was worthless without execution. The BadgerCo leadership team had long held a weekly staff meeting. Once a month, this meeting was re-purposed and dedicated to progress updates on the strategic plan. The team used a simple, status-at-a-glance dashboard. The point person for each initiative gave a brief progress report, focusing on execution challenges that might require a course adjustment or additional resources. These review meetings created a forum for the leadership team to give an honest assessment of progress and hold each other accountable. After a few months, the dashboard needed to be re-stocked as initiatives were completed. Wins were celebrated, lessons learned were shared, and then new projects were added to the list. Through these review meetings, the dashboard became a living document rather than a static list. Over time, the next level of leadership at the company was included in the process. Managers took a more active role in planning, sequencing, and executing initiatives. The result: better decisions, higher ownership, and a company ahead of schedule in achieving its vision.

Strategy Summary

Who are we?

MISSION

BadgerCo supplies and supports the remote installation and service of complex industrial systems for power generation, clean tech, and water filtration markets.

Where are we going?

VISION 2023

By 2023 we will achieve $50 million in net sales with EBITDA margin of over 10%.

We will:
- ✓ Reduce our customer concentration
- ✓ Develop our own product designs
- ✓ Diversify end-market risk
- ✓ Expand credentials & certifications

	Today	2023
Net Sales	$13 mil	$50 mil
Sales to OEM "X"	$10 mil	$15 mil
Water Filtration Rev	-	$5 mil+
Engineering FTEs	4	10
...		
EBITDA Margin	9-11%	>10%

How are we going to get there?

KEY IMPERATIVES

Develop Standard Product Lines	Capture Revenue From Kitting & Testing Services	Diversify End-Market Exposure	Expand Our Sourcing & Engineering Team

Deep Dive on Initiative Format

A. An effective initiative sets a meaningful, attainable, measurable goal

B. Defining a plan of activities is not enough: when activities are not tied to results there is a decreased likelihood that the targeted results will actually be realized

C. Defining a balanced set of measures and targeted results is not enough: the drivers of most measures are not visible; meaning every time a measure goes south, leaders must retrace their steps and determine what activities are off track

D. Leaders need to define initiatives that clearly connect activities to targeted results
   - Example: "Hire 8 additional sales people by the end of Q1 to generate $16 million in additional revenue by year end. (Owner: Tom Jones)"

E. Each initiative should be assigned a single owner and be written to pass the "SMART" test (see boxes at right)

F. The collection of initiatives for a given year should provide a clear picture of how your company will execute its strategies for that year

G. Detailed actions plans may be required for large, complex, or cross-functional initiatives

Single Owner Concept

The owner is not *solely* responsible for the execution of the initiative.

Often a large, cross-functional team is needed to get the job done.

The owner is the point person responsible for managing execution, raising flags, reporting status, and making adjustments as required.

SMART Format

Initiatives should be written so that they pass the "SMART" test.

They should be:
- Specific
- Measurable
- Action-oriented
- Results-based
- Time-bound

Deep Dive on At-A-Glance Dashboard

Imperative	Status	Initiative	Start Date	Due Date	Cost ($000s)	Owner	Support Team
I. Increase market share	A.	Hire eight additional sales people by the end of Q1 to generate $16 million in additional revenue by year end	Jan 1	Dec 31	$1,000	T Jones	HR
	B.						
	C.						
II. Imperative ...	A.						
	B.						
II. Imperative ...	A.						
	B.						
	C.						
	D.						

A. A one-page dashboard is an effective tool for tracking initiatives.
B. Fields in the dashboard can be customized to fit your business needs but should include:
  - Initiative description
  - Start and due dates
  - Cost
  - Owner & support team
  - Status: Darker-Lighter-Medium Gray
C. The senior leadership team should review the dashboard on a regular basis (at least quarterly, often monthly)
D. Discussion time should be focused on items that are stalled or off track (darker or lighter gray) so that decisions to adjust course or allocate additional/different resources can be made

Takeaways from the Case Study

1. Sustained success requires a compelling strategy to provide context for execution.
2. The "Strategic Framework" clearly describes who you are (Mission), where you are going (Vision) and how you are going to get there (Key Imperatives & Supporting Key Initiatives)

3. An initiative defines a corporate priority and establishes a commitment to execute.
4. Engaging the "next level of leaders" can improve the quality of the plan and build front-line ownership.
5. Regular progress management (reviewing status, adjusting course, shifting resources) keeps the plan relevant and improves odds of success.
6. Less is more: accomplishing a few critical priorities year after year is more effective than creating long lists of priorities and accomplishing few of them.

Driving Competitive Strategy Through A Private Company's Board

As previously noted, the primary functions of boards of directors include oversight, strategy, succession planning, capital structure, and risk management. Strategy, capital structure, and succession planning are the responsibilities that a board manages to create value, while oversight and risk management are more often seen as ways to protect the enterprise.

Strategy has been defined as the art of finding an unfair competitive advantage in the marketplace. It is implemented through defined objectives and tactics. Whether public or private, driving strategy is how boards create value. Public companies tend to have well-staffed strategy groups, with M&A being one component. Private companies tend to be simpler.

The goal of a public company is to maximize shareholder value, which today means an increase in the stock price. The quarterly treadmill drives behaviors. Private companies can invest for longer horizons, so their strategic horizon is typically much longer than that of a public company.

Private companies with greater than a few hundred million dollars in revenue move along an evolutionary path resembling public company strategy functions. But most private companies are smaller than $100 million revenue and have no formal strategy function. They are focused on surviving and hopefully prospering in a single market.

Fundamentals Of Private Company Strategy

For private companies, strategy really means "what do you want to do with your business?" Private companies do not answer to outside parties, except their lenders and the IRS. Since there are typically only one or two opinions that matter, if the owners are happy, that is good enough.

I submit that private company strategy can be summed up by three questions:

What are the owners' goals for the business? Defining the owners' goals usually happens through a visioning exercise: what do you want the company to look like in five years? This usually turns into a desired set of financial statements, some market share and product descriptors, and a few qualitative statements, e.g., "most desired employer".

There is a well-understood process for moving from a visioning exercise to a full strategic plan. From the board's perspective, it needs to include answers to these questions:

- Does the board have a plan on how to allocate profits between funding growth, paying down debt, tax distributions, and spendable distributions to owners?
- Are cash balances disproportionately high compared to monthly fixed costs?
- Does the dividend policy meet the needs of the owners?
- Are there external capital sources (banks) to support your capital structure?
- Does management have a strong grip on growth opportunities in adjacent markets?
- Is there an open discussion on how much risk the board and ownership will accept?

If the owners do not have significant experience outside their own business, they may not know they need to comprehensively ask and answer these questions. That is why it is common for outside directors to lead on these issues at a private company.

How do you translate the owners' goals into the budget, dividend policy, and capital structure? Many companies have completed thorough strategy exercises to produce a nice report that is then put on the shelf. Market forces will drive management behavior if not managed by the board. Capital should be allocated to the highest and best uses to achieve the owners' goals. Performance incentives need to support the corporate goals. Setting priorities means killing pet projects that are outside the strategy.

Outside directors often need to be the "adult in the room" when it comes to forcing the budget to reflect priorities. This usually does not happen naturally.

How do you measure progress towards the owners' goals? Budgets alone are not sufficient to measure progress in pursuing a strategy. The board needs to develop metrics and measurables, e.g., KPI, dashboard, etc., that best speak to progress on strategic imperatives. Budget numbers and financials are not sufficiently indicative for this purpose.

Metrics And Measurables

These metrics should be developed with management to assure their full buy-in for what they will be held accountable. Well-run boards will have an end-to-end process that drives management and staff behavior to be fully aligned with ownership goals, with accountability.

Good leadership will translate these KPIs from the company level to management performance appraisals and down to staff appraisals. They should already be tied to the budget and capital expenditure program. Once developed, these KPIs need to be the live or die metrics going forward. This is a primary method for boards to hold management accountable.

The transparency of the public markets drives the accountability that is often lacking in private companies. This is where outside directors often make the difference in private company governance.

If you serve on a private company board, you should be working to understand, evaluate, and improve the company's strategy. This is one of the ways you demonstrate your value as a director.

If you are considering joining a private company board, you should evaluate their strategy process to understand how the board functions, and its impact on the business.

An important job of the board is to assist with developing a competitive strategy. To quote wise King Solomon, "For by wise counsel you will wage your own war, and in a multitude of counselors there is safety."[14]

Oftentimes the wise counsel of the board is invaluable to craft competitive strategy.

How To Build A Competitive Strategy That Works For You

Many business owners think of strategy as complicated, where consultants create eighty-page PowerPoint decks to explain what they should do and why. In larger public companies, this is often true since the forces at play are so complex and intertwined.

Yet most private companies have only a few product lines, pursue limited channels of distribution, are confined to a domestic reach, and are capital and/or management constrained. This reduces the difficulty of creating an effective competitive strategy. If revenue is generated mostly through e-commerce, the strategy questions are even simpler.

While we have been led to believe that a competitive strategy needs to be complicated, most private companies' history has shown that a simpler approach is likely to be more impactful. You should be able to articulate your growth strategy in just a few pages, and it should be easy for everyone in the organization to understand.

After all, they are the people who have to do the work. You want them to easily connect the big picture to their daily activities. This approach creates organizational leverage and enhances their engagement by making their efforts more meaningful.

Army companies have between sixty and two hundred soldiers, since at that size, one captain could manage those relationships. This may or may not be true in your organization. The biggest challenge of leadership is to deliver business results through others, especially when there is no personal relationship or direct communication to rely upon. Remote work makes this even more challenging.

A succinct, well-developed strategy document is as much a communications tool as it is a business planning event. Here is what it should look like.

Include Well-Defined Goals Set By Owners

Business owners are responsible for providing directives to the board and management on what they expect the business to achieve and what constraints they wish to impose on how the business operates.

Metrics should include revenue, EBITDA (earnings before interest, taxes, depreciation, and amortization), increased valuation, market share, or something similarly concrete. When this information is confidential, translate it into the operational metrics already in use. Whenever possible, goals should be SMART (specific, measurable, achievable, relevant, and time-bound).

Have A Time Frame To Measure Results

It is hard to plan much past three to five years, as the world will change your situation by then. If ownership sets a five-year objective, break it down into annual steps. It is hard to solve a complicated problem in one step. So break it down into smaller, more solvable problems, and then roll up your results. Years become quarters, quarters become months, and months become weeks.

Strategy needs to be linked to tactics, from top to bottom.

Annual and quarterly business goals need to be broken down into the quarterly, monthly, weekly, and daily tasks for each decision-maker in the organization. Everyone from top to bottom needs to be connected.

You will want to do this in concert with the people you are relying on since you need their buy-in to get results. Have these discussions to identify the constraints on growth, and then do something to remove those constraints.

Make sure your strategy:

- **Is consistent with the company's culture and persona.** Organizations don't usually tolerate decisions that conflict with their inherent

values. You know who you are, for better or worse. Don't fight your own DNA.
- **Is crafted for what the management team can actually get done.** Once you figure out what needs to get done, be realistic about what can be done. If you lack the talent or bandwidth, figure that out first before launching a campaign that is destined to go nowhere fast.
- **Holds management accountable.** Traditionally, management develops a strategy to be reviewed and approved by the board. Ownership has given a clear mandate to the board on what it expects from the business. Then the board holds management accountable for delivering the approved plan. If these bodies are the same few people, who ensures accountability? For smaller organizations, this is often the most difficult issue to grapple with.
- **Provides a timely feedback loop.** One of the shortcomings of the MS PowerPoint method is that the reports have a short half-life. A strategy piece should be a living document; it evolves over time as conditions change. An annual review is always a good starting point but may not make sense for your industry. What is the rate of change in your industry? Be sure to stay ahead of it.

In business school, many of us learned that strategy development is a fixed process, then deployed into action. But for most private companies, it is more important to take action, learn, and adjust in real time. If you maintain pace, you have time to adjust without taking too much risk. This is why most software is now developed with the Agile or Scrum method versus the traditional project planning method.

Strategy development and execution is a process, not an event. Someone needs to manage the overall process since everyone already has a full-time job. That may be the most important decision of all when it comes to strategy.

Another important issue is that strategy needs to include resilience to overcome adversity. Reflecting on his efforts to end apartheid in South Africa,

Nelson Mandela said: "Do not judge me by my success, judge me by how many times I fell down and got back up."

The board plays a key role in business resilience, which is an underpinning of a great competitive strategy.

Assessing And Improving Business Resilience

Business resilience is a concept with a new meaning in the post-pandemic world. It has been defined by NACD as: "the capacity of any entity to prepare for disruptions, to recover from shocks and stresses, and then to adapt and grow from a disruptive experience." Resilience is the demonstrated ability to "bounce forward better." Numerous technical standards give their own definitions of resilience, such as ISO 22316:2017, which defines organizational resilience as:

> *The ability of an organization to absorb and adapt in a changing environment to enable it to deliver its objectives and to survive and prosper.*

Within the world of technology, ITIL 4 defines resilience as the ability of an organization to anticipate, prepare for, respond to, and adapt to both incremental changes and sudden disruptions from an external perspective. Similar to NACD, it means being able to take a blow, recover, and move forward.

Disaster recovery plans are associated with security breaches, fires, and hurricanes. But resilience is about survival and adaptation. Darwin's famous quote is "survival of the most adaptable" not "survival of the fittest." If you take a moment to ponder the difference between "fitness" and "adaptability" it should be clear they are not the same concepts.

If you are running a business today, you have likely lived through October 1987, 9/11, 2008, and now a global pandemic. Black swan events are a part of life, just not everyday occurrences. We should expect them.

When you comb through the numerous definitions and examples of business resilience, what stands out is that it is about how a group of people deal with adversity, communicate on priorities and risks, and make decisions and move forward despite a lack of information, amid great uncertainty, and likely in great peril.

Resilience is an absolute measure of the management team's ability to manage change and uncertainty. There is a reason why people say, "it's all about the people." Leadership needs to be able to manage the team in the moment, much as a captain steers a ship through a storm. To be better prepared for the next event, ask yourself these three questions:

What did your team do better than expected during these stress periods?

You should get input from your team on this one. The examples will be more diverse. Get the input, and then synthesize what the numerous examples really point out. Was it just a few heroes solving the big problems, or did everyone pull together?

Critically, listen for what people are *not* saying. That is usually the most important takeaway from this type of exercise. For example, do you hear, "Wow, the leadership really stepped up and showed us the way forward. We could not have done it without them?" Or "We were really scared about what was going to happen, but working with our management made a bad situation much easier to deal with." If you are not hearing this, why not?

Where were you blindsided when you should have been prepared? If so, do you understand why? Was it due to systemic issues or unrelated causes? Were they foreseeable at all? What was the flaw in your risk management system that caused these issues to be surprises, and what part of the system is so broken that it allowed this to happen? If the cause of the issue is within the boardroom and not the management team, how is the board getting the feedback and being held accountable to protect ownership?

What aspects of your culture and governance need to improve so you have greater resilience in the future? Everyone knows culture is the straw that stirs the business's drink, but there are no obvious levers to pull to make changes. Especially with culture, change has to come from the top of the organization. The old saw is that "children watch what you do, not what you say" and that is also true in a business setting.

Introspection and the ability to challenge yourself with intellectual honesty are the hallmarks of critical thinking. It requires discipline and is likely to be uncomfortable, but it needs to be done.

What's Next

Strategy and tactics are critical, but people make it happen. What happens when you need to have people in the wings ready to step up when necessary? This will be considered in the following chapter on succession.

Chapter 9 Takeaways

Board Function: Strategy Development And Execution

Understand strategy development and execution is a process, not an event. Someone needs to manage the overall process since everyone already has a full-time job. That may be the most important decision of all when it comes to strategy.

Realize strategy needs to be consistent with the company's culture and persona. Organizations don't usually tolerate decisions that conflict with their inherent values. You know who you are, for better or worse. Don't fight your own DNA.

Know what the management team can actually get done. Once you figure out what needs to get done, be realistic about what can be done. If you lack the talent or bandwidth, figure that out first before launching a campaign that is destined to go nowhere.

Boards should hold management accountable. Ownership should give a clear mandate to the board on what it expects from the business. Traditionally, management develops a strategy to be reviewed and approved by the board. Then the board holds management accountable for delivering the approved plan. If these bodies are the same few people, who ensures accountability? For smaller organizations, this can be a difficult issue to grapple with.

Keep the plan current. PowerPoint reports have a short half-life. A strategy manifesto should be a living document; it should evolve over time as conditions change. An annual review is always appropriate, but be sure to stay in sync with the rate of change in your industry.

10

Board Function: Management Succession Planning

An online Harris Poll survey among 502 US business owners with fewer than three hundred employees revealed that almost half of those without a succession plan do not have one because business owners simply believe it is not necessary (47 percent).[15]

Other reasons business owners neglect succession planning include not wanting to give up one's life work (14 percent), not knowing when to create a plan (11 percent) or who to work with (11 percent), not having time to develop a plan (11 percent), and being overwhelmed with government regulations (8 percent).

"Business owners function at such a rapid pace to remain competitive so it's no wonder that developing their exit plan and replacement doesn't seem like today's priority," noted Kirt Walker, then president & COO of Nationwide Financial. "Yet, there isn't a more critical component of an operational plan than a solid business succession plan for providing seamless continuity in a time of crisis or transition."

It's never too late to begin management succession planning. Here is some advice to help you get started as soon as possible.

Identify Your Business Objectives To Determine Management Succession Needs

One of the primary responsibilities of a board of directors is to provide management continuity. Emergencies tend to resolve themselves since decisions can't wait. Proactive management succession planning is the hallmark of a well-run organization and is more demanding than just pondering who the next CEO will be.

It all starts with having a clear business strategy and then understanding the future leadership requirements. Then, work backward to build the succession plan. If you don't know where you are going, how do you know how to get there?

This chart maps out the overall process:

Business Objectives Drive Talent Needs
Succession plan is driven by where you want to go

Business Objectives → Future Talent Need → Assess Current Staff → Gap Analysis → Development Plans for Current Staff / Recruiting Needs → Transition Timeline

- Capital Need
- Skill/Will
- Job Descriptions & Deliverables
- Compensation
- Development Plans
- Monitor Results & Adjust to Goal

Figure 8

Understanding your future talent requirements means identifying the future business objectives and designing the organization to get there. From there you need to:

- Consider the skills and experiences needed to achieve those goals. Success is usually determined by cultural fit, style, and experience.

- Realize filling positions is often a trade-off between "must haves" and "wanna haves." The pivot is typically made when you decide what you can and can't live without.
- Assess the current staff needs to include their interpersonal skills and cultural fit regardless of the past. Do they align with the business vision? Can you quantify past performance with data, or is it just a collection of biased opinions? Were the past performance appraisals thorough and fair?
- Understand that the Skill/Will matrix is a quick and simple tool to assess your current talent.[16] Developed in the 1970s, it segments people by their expertise and their desire to be successful. Each quadrant requires different types of supervision and development.

Figuring Out What You Need

In your future organization, there are likely new positions to be created, and thus new job descriptions written and rated for compensation purposes. For your current staff, what development do they need to acquire the skills and experience to fill those roles? If you lack the internal talent needed to staff the future organization, you need to go outside.

To determine where you stand, you should complete a gap analysis once you've taken these steps:

1. Decide where you are headed.
2. Discover the skills and experiences leaders must possess to achieve your business objectives.
3. Evaluate your current staff.

The gap analysis should involve these questions:

- What is the difference between what you need and what you have?
- With development, can the internal candidates meet future expectations? If not, you need to go outside to fill the gaps.

Management Succession Timelines

Transition timelines should be developed in detail, since at this point management succession tends to mean applying thorough project management skills. If you don't identify the details, assign duties and deadlines, and track them religiously, time will slip by and a smooth succession may not happen on time or at all.

Developing the timelines often means working backward from an immovable deadline, such as a planned retirement. When does the candidate need to be in the new job and fully up to speed? How long will it take to train them and backfill their current position? How long will it take to recruit and onboard the backfilled positions? When do you have to start this chain of events?

Thoughtful Communication

Dealing with potential conflicts early and directly is usually best, as these things do not get better on their own.

Since this impacts people's careers and livelihoods, thoughtful communication is critical. Who needs to know what and when without creating a rumor mill? Certainly, the future leaders need to be brought along early. But people who are likely to be disappointed with the results need to be treated with dignity and respect.

Management succession is both a process and a project to be managed. It takes time and energy and should not be rushed. Give yourself enough time to figure it out and likely three to five years to execute.

But what happens if the succession plan goes horribly wrong? There are choices to make to revive a succession plan on the rocks.

Options To Revive A Failed Succession Plan

The final test of a great business leader is to pass the reins to a successor and see the business continue to prosper. This may be more difficult in professional service firms since leadership and revenue are tightly linked.

Transferring client relationships to a successor can be challenging. Failing to do this well may cause the firm to falter, or worse.

In a recent client situation, this was exactly the problem that needed to be solved. The firm was successful for several decades. But as the founding partners approached their natural retirement age, their succession plans became obsolete. The partner who generated most of the revenue passed away very unexpectedly. The other partner was able to maintain the status quo, but the firm ceased to grow and settled, a bit too comfortably, into a stagnant status quo. Then the firm became paralyzed, with declining productivity.

The partner loved the business and wanted to protect the employees. He felt a self-imposed moral obligation not to sell the firm to a large, impersonal competitor. But he soon realized he was trapped between forces he could no longer control. He wanted to retire, but there was no one who could sustain revenue. While he had developed good managers, there was no one coming up who could be developed into a successor within his timeframe to retire. He felt trapped with no good way forward.

Fortunately, there is always another way. To create a viable succession plan, I asked these questions: (1) Can we recruit a senior hire who could become a rainmaker by the time the partner wanted to retire? (2) Can we reposition the firm to be an employer-of-choice to attract the talent needed to get the firm back into a growth mode? (3) What investments can be made to drive growth? The intention was to develop a plan to provide for succession so the partner would not be forced to sell.

Since the partner needed to exit from management and ownership, I asked him to think about these issues:

- Is your priority to maximize economic value, achieve some non-monetary goal, or strike a balance between competing objectives?
- Do you have the time and desire to improve performance, thereby creating more value before exiting?
- What are the timeline and influencing factors, e.g., health, lifestyle changes, that influence the likely options?

Given these needs, here is the process we suggested to develop a path forward:

1. Establish the value of the firm and how it fits into the partner's retirement planning. Do we need to materially increase the value of the firm to assure a feasible retirement plan?
2. Evaluate the current talent pool for possible successors. Let's rate and rank individuals to decide if there is at least an 85 percent chance of being able to groom a successor within the time available.
3. If there is no likely successor, we needed to evaluate if the partner should invest time and money to reposition the firm, hire a successor, and rebuild the staff. This is normally a three- to five-year process if successful. It is also a high risk since there are so many variables involved.
4. If that is not a viable path, a sales transaction becomes inevitable. The goal would be to manage a sales process that attracts buyers who are more likely to take care of the employees in the future.

One benefit of this discussion is that the partner realized he was underinvesting in the business development process. Regardless of the succession plan, more could be done to drive revenue, which always helps. Working with the partner, we spent time developing a more effective sales and marketing program, did a better job managing the business development pipeline, took a harder look at costs, created better incentives to improve productivity, and spent more energy communicating with customers and staff about the firm's competitive advantages.

The end result after six months was that a new succession plan was developed, allowing the partner to sleep better at night. While it was not what he originally expected, it did meet his needs and allow him to retire comfortably and proudly by passing responsibility to a new leadership team.

Even in a family business, sometimes succession means going outside the family. Learn from the experience of others if this is the case for you.

Ten Tips For Hiring Your First Non-Family CEO

Transitioning to a new CEO is always challenging. Doing so in a multigenerational family business is harder. But hiring the first non-family executive to run a family business may be the riskiest type of CEO succession. There are only a few ways for things to go right, but an infinite number of ways for them to go wrong.

While you have likely heard numerous stories about failed successions, you may not have heard of the many successful transitions that have occurred in family-owned businesses.

What are the secrets to success? Here are some suggestions for how to get it right the first time.

Everyone must agree on the candidate. The selection decision needs to be an agreement, preferably a unanimous one. As with many decisions in the boardroom, it is acceptable to strongly disagree during the decision-making process, but once a decision is made, everyone needs to visibly support it for the good of the organization.

Define the new CEO's authority. In most family businesses, there are written and unwritten rules about how things get done. When there is no one to tell the new CEO about the unwritten rules, they tend to find out too late. Worse, this happens while they are trying to develop relationships and build trust.

As part of the hiring process, the company must thoroughly negotiate the decision-making authority of the new CEO. This means determining which decisions they can make alone versus when a discussion needs to happen (with the whole board or the chairperson, whoever the CEO reports to directly) before a decision is made. This determination will be very specific to each company's situation.

By defining the CEO's authority, the organization will come to know who is really in charge. Is the new CEO a "real" CEO, a COO, or just a caretaker while the ownership makes up its mind on what it wants to?

Provide a clear mandate to the new CEO. The ownership group needs to be clear on what it wants this person to accomplish and when. The new

CEO will value their time and likely be ambitious. The mandate will be the key incentive for them to join the organization, as they will want to accomplish something meaningful and not waste their time. The candidates will want a clear statement of what ownership expects them to deliver.

Allow them to build their own relationships. Every CEO needs to develop their own relationships within the organization to get results through collaboration. The family needs to give the new CEO enough runway to figure out who does what, how to motivate them, how things really get done, and what makes the organization tick.

Have a transition timeline. The outgoing CEO needs to consider how they will turn over the reins to their successor. What can be achieved during onboarding? What takes more time? What do you "just have to be there" to understand? Key relationships with customers and suppliers take time. At what point in these relationships does the outgoing CEO stand in front of the new CEO, beside the new CEO, or behind them, and at what point do they walk away?

Provide a simple reporting structure. While the CEO often reports to the board, it is not effective for the CEO to have five to seven people to report to, each of whom might give different marching orders. The board needs to decide on a single point of contact for the CEO and manage its discussions through that one person.

Be clear on how conflicts get resolved. How are conflicts resolved in your organization? How does the process change based on the type of conflict, magnitude of risk, and participants? The more the board makes the CEO guess, the more mistakes they will make.

For family businesses, who is the tiebreaker on key decisions? When the family is deadlocked, do they expect the non-family CEO to be the tiebreaker? While that often happens, it may only be effective after many years of trusted service.

Discuss future ownership composition and its implications. Before taking the job, the leading candidate will want to understand what the ownership group looks like today and what will likely happen in five to ten years. This lets them know who they will be reporting to, their future wants and needs as owners, and how desirable the situation may become. Just as you are interviewing them, the candidates are interviewing you to assess how desirable you are as an employer.

Create the right incentives. A good CEO will want to know how they can benefit from their efforts. Will they be able to purchase equity? Can they earn it? If not, is a phantom equity program available? If not, why? If so, what are the rules? Ownership should have these answers at the start of the recruiting process.

Let them do their job. After developing the transition plan, stick to it. The exiting CEO should disappear for a while—go to Hawaii for a month or something similar—to prove to the organization that the new CEO is really in charge.

The first non-family CEO cannot solve existing family disputes, and that should not be their job. There are other ways of handling those issues. The family needs the new hire to run the business.

Involving Your Executive Team In Succession Planning

Succession planning in a business is always a delicate matter. There is usually a small cadre of loyal, hard-working, non-family executives who are critical to running the business. Often, the CFO or vice president of sales is at the top of the list.

If they have worked for the business for some years, they are likely already talking among themselves about what is going to happen. They know the age and health of the owners, the potential of the children, and the health of the business. You want smart people working for you, and smart people ask good questions.

These people are information gatekeepers. They know what the staff is talking about, especially when no one is willing to raise delicate issues with the owners. These gatekeepers are who the staff go to when they want to know what the family is saying and thinking. These are the responsible employees who answer on behalf of the owners without getting the owners involved in certain conversations.

In many businesses, these few people are the fulcrum of how work gets done. They are the bridge between the "inner sanctum" of discussions and the rank-and-file staff.

With that frame of reference, why would you exclude them from the succession process? Having them as part of the process does not mean they are making decisions. But it is a way to increase the likelihood of a successful transition.

Establish A Communication Plan

One of the most important parts of succession planning is how the owners communicate on the issues. You need to manage the message. People like to gossip, especially when it involves job security. You want to tamp down this energy and get people focused on work. While each situation is different, you need to have a plan and stay ahead of the crowd.

The three parts of a good communication plan are knowing:

1. What to say
2. Who to say it to
3. When to say it

These decisions need to be made before the search process starts because the staff will see strangers coming through the building. They usually figure it out. The candidates will want to meet their future direct reports and ask questions to assess their level of interest in the job.

While the communication plan will need to be flexible and adaptable, you need a starting point.

Consider The Prerequisites To Succession Planning

When a family wants to retain ownership of its business but does not have a successor CEO within the family, it needs to wrestle with the transition. While this requires traditional management succession planning, it also requires the family to prepare itself for owning but not running the business. There are a few cautions to be aware of before engaging in this issue.

First, this is a process to be managed, not a project. Managing the process at the macro level is different from executing the various pieces of it. Second, you may need more than one professional to manage this process, as it requires a variety of skill sets. Good professionals will coordinate their services for the benefit of the client. While cost is always a concern, this work will be spread over months and years. So instead of worrying about the total cost, think about the monthly spend to fund this effort. It is a cost of doing business, and of being a successful family business.

In a recent situation, the family leadership intended to retire within a few years, and there was no succession plan. Further, most of the family members did not save for their retirement, so financial security was a concern. Others were hesitant to retire since they didn't know what they were going to do after leaving the business.

This was a second-generation East Coast service business, and the elderly mother, while not active, still controlled the major decisions even though the adult son and two daughters had been running the business for years. The family had amassed wealth but never spent it.

After working with the family, it became clear three questions would drive the outcome:

- What is the purpose of the wealth? The family had enough wealth that current income was not an issue, but their attitude prevented them from using the wealth for the benefit of the family. Since the working family had not saved for retirement, the obvious answer was to deploy assets to maintain financial security since it would not diminish their portfolio long term. But doing so was emotionally difficult, and that problem had to be solved.
- Do they intend to keep the business when Mom is gone? It is common for the surviving parent to hold the family together, and then the family falls apart after their departure. The business usually gets sold

since the controlling family members can't work together effectively. So if the siblings wanted to keep the business for their heirs they had to work together without Mom's oversight and coercion.

- How do they expect to make decisions when Mom no longer does? This is the tough issue. They needed to develop mechanisms to make tough decisions, without Mom being the tiebreaker. This tends to be a binary issue. We needed to wrestle with these macro issues first to make the working family comfortable to proceed with succession planning.

Here were the issues to solve next:

Financial security for retiring family leadership. The simple solution was to distribute the amounts equal to their after-tax W-2 income from their investment portfolio. Since this was less than 3 percent of the portfolio, we knew it was not a major financial risk for the family. That was the easy part. Maintaining the discipline to not increase distributions above that level was a concern. The business was nicely profitable. In addition to the nominal retirement plans, we examined a supplemental retirement plan for the family members. These two methods allowed us to provide financial security without overburdening the business or the portfolio.

Personal transition plans. Family members will be reluctant to leave if they don't know where they are going. We had discussions on what their daily life would be like in retirement. We focused on their joys and identified and hedged their fears. We created a personal transition plan for each individual. We had to make sure they were excited about where they were going and not overly focused on what they were leaving.

Governance processes. The business did not have a board of advisors or formal board of directors since Mom made the decisions. They came to understand that over the next few years, the entire management team would be non-family, and they needed a mechanism to protect ownership via proper oversight and controls. The first step was to create a board of advisors, with outsiders, so the family became used to having outsiders involved in key issues. It was agreed that when there was no family in the business, the board would evolve into a fiduciary board. We also knew a strong fiduciary board would help in recruiting top talent since it would insulate the new management from family issues.

Once this was in place, the individuals felt secure and empowered to step back and transition to new management with governance. No change in ownership was required. This approach also allowed the family to consider equity-linked incentives to secure good talent.

What's Next

Are you familiar with the Boy Scout motto, Be Prepared?

> *The Scout motto means that you are always ready to do what is necessary to help others. It also means you are ready, willing, and able to do what is necessary in any situation that comes along.*[17]

Being prepared with an exit plan and succession plan needs to be a priority. A solid business succession plan will provide seamless continuity in a time of crisis or transition.

Now let's examine another critical area where preparedness pays off, and that is capital structure.

Chapter 10 Takeaways

Board Function: Management Succession Planning

Identify your management succession needs. One of the primary responsibilities of a board is to provide management continuity. Emergencies tend to resolve themselves since decisions can't wait. Proactive succession planning is the hallmark of a well-run organization.

Go all-in with the planning process. It starts with having a clear business strategy that drives your future leadership needs. Start with the answer and work backward. Succession planning is both a process and a project to be managed.

Know your timing. There is likely an immovable deadline to meet, such as a retirement. Give yourself enough time to figure it out.

Realize that thoughtful, timely communications are key. Who needs to know what, when, and why? Sometimes, what you don't say may be as important as what you do say.

Provide a clear mandate to the new CEO. The ownership group needs to be clear on what it wants this person to accomplish and when. The new CEO will value their time and be ambitious. They will want to accomplish something meaningful and not waste their time.

Have a transition timeline. The outgoing CEO needs to consider how they will turn over the reins to their successor. What can be achieved during onboarding? What takes more time? What do you "just have to be there" to understand? Key relationships with customers and suppliers take time. At what point in these relationships does the outgoing CEO stand in front of the new CEO, beside the new CEO, or behind them, and at what point do they walk away?

Let them do their job. After developing the transition plan, stick to it. The exiting CEO should disappear for a while—go to Hawaii for a month or something similar—to prove to the organization that the new CEO is really in charge.

11

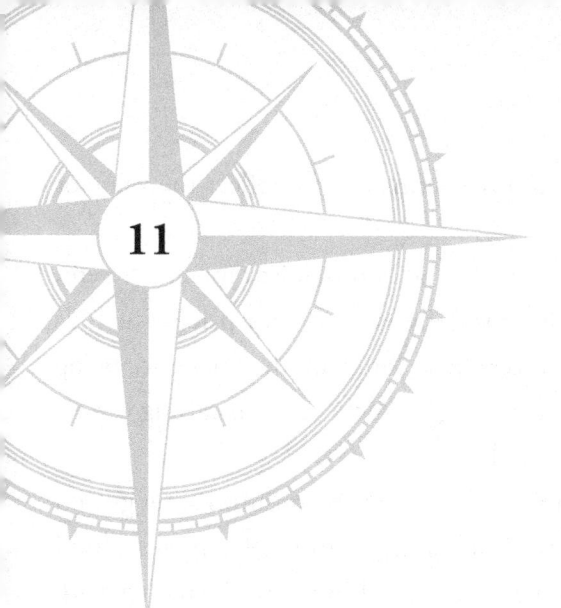

Board Function: Capital Structure

Business is the confluence of people, money, ideas, and opportunities. You need to get all four in the right proportions to achieve commercial success. Money is a commodity. Whether it is debt or equity, how it is structured reflects how impactful the combination of people, ideas, and opportunities are.

Having spent years working in the venture capital and private equity arenas, I have heard too often people complain about how hard it is to raise capital for their business. But they have it backward.

Since General Georges Doriot started the venture capital industry in 1946, the truth has been that the market tends to fund worthy ideas and pass on the others. The capital markets are relatively efficient in that way, although they are certainly not perfect either.[18]

When people complain, "If only I had the money," they are saying they are not presenting the market with something deserving the risk capital they are asking to be trusted with.

Raising Capital

Funding sources need to know you have a long-term competitive advantage in a well-defined market and you deeply understand your customers' wants and needs and how much they will pay for your products and services.

Their desire to provide funding and the terms thereof reflect the value of what you are doing.

When you think about trading stocks and bonds, it isn't much different. On a financial exchange, everything is defined except for price. The bids and asks are the price discovery process in action, with the final price being the definition of fair value of that trade. This is the same as raising capital for your business but on a micro level.

The three steps to raising capital are: (1) set the business strategy and detailed planning, (2) decide how much and the form of capital to fund the plan, and (3) demonstrate you can be trusted to return the money with a risk-adjusted amount of profit.

No one's going to give you money without details on your sources and uses of capital. So you must be prepared to share your plan—a plan that allows the providers to get their money back with a risk-adjusted profit because without that, no one will give you the money.

You also must have a capital structure that lets you sleep at night. Because when sales drop 20 percent, e.g., due to COVID-19, and the bank starts calling, some owners don't have the stomach for it. If sales drop and your equity investors start calling, this old phrase may come to mind: success has a thousand fathers and failure is an orphan.[19]

TOTAL CAPITALIZATION

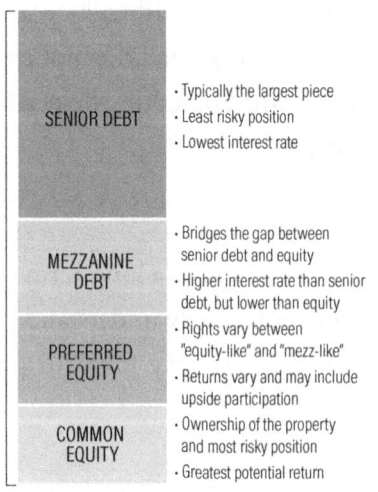

SENIOR DEBT	• Typically the largest piece • Least risky position • Lowest interest rate
MEZZANINE DEBT	• Bridges the gap between senior debt and equity • Higher interest rate than senior debt, but lower than equity
PREFERRED EQUITY	• Rights vary between "equity-like" and "mezz-like" • Returns vary and may include upside participation
COMMON EQUITY	• Ownership of the property and most risky position • Greatest potential return

Figure 9

Your capital structure includes all the capital used to support the business, including all debt and equity. Each structure has several variations—preferred equity, common stock, senior debt, junior debt, mezzanine lending, and structured equity, as noted in Figure 9. The goal is to have an efficient capital structure, which gives you the best return for the level of risk you're willing to accept.

As you move from bottom to top of the capital stack, you have more security. Think about it; the government always gets its taxes before anyone else gets paid, right? And employees are protected by law for their wages. In most states, both are a personal liability of the owners.

But as you move from top to bottom, the rewards of ownership increase. Bondholders get their principal and interest but nothing more. The common owners get the most upside since they have taken the most risk.

Successfully executing a business strategy requires capital and talent; let's examine both in detail.

Money Is A Raw Material

When you buy raw materials for your business, you usually look for the lowest cost for your specified need. You know what a pound of steel costs or how much it costs to ship a container from Shanghai to Los Angeles. Capital isn't much different; it is just another input. So shouldn't you try to get the lowest cost of capital?

A firm's total cost of capital is a weighted average of the cost of equity and the cost of debt, known as the weighted average cost of capital (WACC).

The formula for WACC looks complicated but is simple if you think it through:

$$WACC = (E/V \times Re) + ((D/V \times Rd) \times (1 - T))$$

Where:
E = market value of the firm's equity (market cap)
V = total value of capital (equity plus debt)
E/V = percentage of capital that is equity

R_e = cost of equity (required rate of return)
D = market value of the firm's debt
D/V = percentage of capital that is debt
R_d = cost of debt (yield to maturity on existing debt)
T = tax rate

To break it down further, you need to focus on:

- What rate of return do my equity investors require to reward the risk they are taking?
- If I am selling equity, how much of my business am I willing to give up?
- What interest rate does my bank demand to give me the loans I want?
- How much debt can the business handle so I can still sleep at night?

Owners need to weigh these tradeoffs such that they have the capital needed to fund their business plan and enough margin of safety so if business gets soft, they comply with their debt covenants.

A Board Member's Perspective On Raising Capital

As previously noted, boards are responsible for oversight, strategy, management succession, capital structure, and risk management. Most of their time tends to focus on strategy and management. Once a business strategy is developed, it is then about finding the capital to fund growth and securing the talent to execute the plan.

The outside directors, or advisors, will tend to be strong in strategy and execution. But I find fewer of them are likely to have deep experience in the capital markets unless they were specifically recruited to provide that knowledge.

Most private companies don't need to raise capital often, except for routine commercial loans. Hence, it is unlikely that they will have significant capital raising experience in the boardroom or executive suite.

Fortunately, most of the skills and experience needed to raise capital can be rented from investment bankers, lawyers, and consultants. Even with that convenience, the ownership—and the board, if there is one—needs to understand the fundraising process. While they don't need to be experts in the marketing process, they do need to focus on the decisions that cannot be delegated to outside professionals.

Having watched numerous clients go through this process, here is my advice to help bring this into focus.

Have Clear Goals

What needs to get done, and why is it important? When does it need to happen? A short fundraising strategy document, driven by ownership objectives, should be created.

A typical directive might be: "We need to raise $10 million of equity within twelve months to fund our five-year growth plan. About $4 million of that amount is to fund acquisitions and the rest is to drive organic growth in the current plus two new markets." This is your North Star during the process.

What are your non-negotiable terms? Are you willing to give up control? Does the new capital partner get to pick the next CEO or a few board seats, or are they expected to be fully passive? You will need to make tradeoffs so be sure to know what you are unwilling to give away.

Once you enter the fundraising process, you might experience an ongoing series of surprises. They may be good or bad, but they need to be dealt with. You need that North Star to guide you through the turbulence. If you don't identify clear goals upfront, you can make a difficult task that much harder.

Understand The Market

You need to understand what the capital markets have to offer and what your business offers to them. Each potential investor has different expectations for IRR, yield, risk, and governance requirements. Take some time to understand these differences and why they are so. You need to understand their motivations and constraints before soliciting interest.

Once you have a good feel for the marketplace, revisit your goals and non-negotiables. Then you can start the fundraising process.

Timing Matters

The financial press often talks about the IPO market opening and closing. This is because it is one of the most volatile—and newsworthy—parts of the market. But the same is true for each segment of the equity and debt markets. Economic cycles, fiscal and monetary policy, and current events drive the millions of individual decisions that make the capital markets.

Raising capital typically becomes a six- to twelve-month process. You need to plan ahead in case the market decides to close just before you plan to enter it.

Intermediary Or Direct?

For many private companies, raising capital means securing a term loan or line of credit from a local bank. Sometimes it means selling a small piece of the business to a trusted friend or relative. Those types of transactions likely just need a good lawyer to get a deal done.

But for larger sums or more complicated situations, the capital will be sourced from someone you don't yet know, like, and trust. How do you find them? If you have direct relationships, you should consider exploring the market if you have the time and confidence to do so. If not, that is why there are intermediaries.

Whether it is an investment bank or business broker, these market participants are critical in keeping the capital markets working. They are the grease between the gears. Some people choose to buy or sell their house by themselves, but most people don't. Raising capital is just not the type of thing where you want to learn from your mistakes, especially when most mistakes are easily avoidable.

Intermediaries should give you a broad exposure to the market while helping you to identify the part of the market best suited to your needs. One aspect of picking an intermediary is to make sure their relationships are broad enough to cover the parts of the market that appeal to you.

What part of this process is run by management versus the board? As with most things in life, it depends. Board members should be able to make introductions to intermediaries and capital sources. They should help with diligence and determining which professionals to engage.

Board members should be the mainstays for disciplining the process, protecting shareholders' interests, and managing conflicts between parties. This is why I believe the most important attribute of a good board member is judgment.

Strategy Drives Cash Allocation

For most businesses, managing cash is a challenge. Margin pressure, seasonality, credit risk, and bank covenants make it a constant chore. Cash is the oxygen of business; you can't run low and survive.

For successful businesses, the opposite is true. They have too much cash. Apple is a well-discussed example; the public markets will force a resolution to its cash hoard. Successful private companies have a more complex problem to solve. Without access to public markets, and without having to answer to anyone but themselves, this is truly a strategic issue.

A client has built a successful business over two generations and has accumulated significant cash on their balance sheet. The client does not need this cash for operations. Being conservative, they always saved for the future. Unless they find a major acquisition, this cash is not a productive asset for the family. They should find a better use for it or return the cash to shareholders. These funds can be used to:

- Fund strategic growth initiatives
- Invest in diversifying strategies
- Pay down debt

- Increase compensation
- Provide peace of mind
- Support charitable causes

In this case, the family had achieved substantial success without having a formal strategic planning process. They were in one industry, were excellent operators, and remained tightly focused on their niche. That is why the cash accumulated over decades.

But as the competitive landscape changed, there were concerns that the future would not be as kind to them as the past had been. New regulations were causing concern. The next generation of leaders had different views than the founder. Some wanted to diversify revenue streams to reduce their risk. Others wanted to take more cash out of the business for personal use. Some were more aggressive than others in pursuing growth opportunities.

Boards are stewards of the owners' capital and should avoid underutilizing assets and taking unwarranted risks. Sound business strategy and ownership priorities should drive how cash is allocated.

The outside directors organized two parallel processes to help the family manage the issues. First, a traditional strategic planning process was started to help set priorities. Simply put, the family needed to set long-term priorities for the business. Fortunately, the family council was effective at this task.

Second, the board formed an investment committee to find professional money managers worthy of managing this large sum of money. The outside directors used their experience to run a competition to find the best managers for the family's situation. Personal chemistry was as much a part of the process as the mechanics of investing.

The board then connected the strategic priorities to the investment management program so the investment policy (risk levels, distributions, volatility) supported the strategic priorities.

Good acquisition opportunities were few and far between in this industry. Having ample cash to be able to move quickly was important to winning.

This was included in developing the investment program—they could move to cash quickly if needed, with no strings attached.

The younger generation was in their forties, so they had a lot of time to put this money to work. But this is where being too conservative may become a liability. Over long time periods, not taking enough risk can become very expensive, since lost opportunities compound just as fast as the market grows. Educating the family on market dynamics allowed decision-makers to define an investment strategy that supported the strategic priorities of the business, provided ample cash flow, allowed the older generation to sleep easy, and excited the younger generation about future potential.

The money managers also provided financial planning for the family members. This assisted with the transition between the generations since each family executive now had a good idea of their personal situation. The guesswork was removed and the executives could focus on the business. This also took some stress out of family relations.

This is a good example of how outside directors can help owners, even highly successful owners, maximize opportunities and manage risk. Too much cash is a good problem to have but a problem nonetheless.

What's Next

Board members can also play an important role in risk management, which is examined in the next chapter.

Chapter 11 Takeaways

Board Function: Capital Structure

Focus on raising capital. Boards are responsible for oversight, strategy, management succession, capital structure, and risk management. Most of their time tends to focus on strategy and management. Once a business strategy is developed, it is then about finding the capital to fund growth and securing the talent to execute the plan.

Understand the market. You need to understand what the capital markets have to offer and what your business offers to them. Each potential investor has different expectations for IRR, yield, risk, and governance requirements. Take some time to understand these differences and why they are so. You need to understand their motivations and constraints before soliciting interest.

Plan far enough ahead. Raising capital typically becomes a six- to twelve-month process. You need to plan ahead in case the market decides to close just before you plan to enter it.

Board members should help to make introductions to intermediaries and capital sources. They should help with diligence and determining which professionals to engage. Board members should be the anchors for disciplining the process, protecting shareholders' interests, and managing conflicts between parties.

Consider you might just need a good lawyer. For some private companies, raising capital means securing a term loan or line of credit from a local bank. Sometimes it means selling a small piece of the business to a trusted friend or relative. Those types of transactions likely just need a good lawyer to get a deal done.

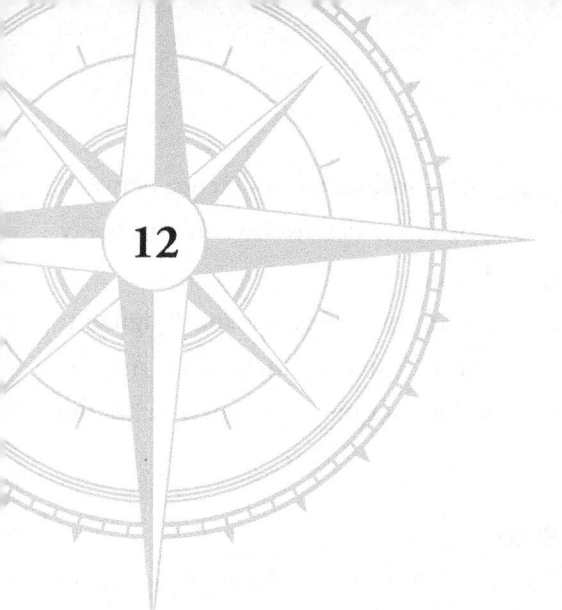

Board Function: Risk Management

Consider the risky situation known as a black swan event. Although talked about in poetry, for much of history black swans were presumed not to exist.

All swans were presumed to be white until 1697 when a Dutch explorer saw swans with dark plumage in Australia, a land largely unexplored by Europeans at that time. "The black swan thus came to be a metaphor for the reality that just because something has not happened does not mean that it cannot occur in the future."[20]

How can you think about possible black swan events when you are struggling with today's problems? Most business owners are so busy running their business they don't have time to think about unlikely events or manage business risks.

To protect shareholders, boards and management need to make time to think about the causes, frequency, and severity of unusual events. For a business to endure for decades, the leadership needs to expect and plan for the unexpected. A risk management plan will help your company do just that.

Unlike an investment, which drives revenue or reduces costs, risk management programs are not just about the numbers. It is easier to justify an investment when you can measure the benefit. It is hard to write a check for something that is unlikely to happen. Consider the difference between buying insurance, backup generators, or cyber defenses when you really want to spend more on marketing and sales.

The key drivers in risk management are risk tolerance and judgment. These vary widely from person to person. A management team may be cohesive and high performing, but that does not mean each person has the same risk tolerance.

How To Best Examine Business Risks

In a recent situation, the outside directors led the board through an exercise to define, qualify, rate, and rank the major threats to the business. These risks included:

- Regulatory changes
- Supplier pressures
- Natural disasters (or biological ones)
- Cybersecurity
- Loss of a key person
- Technology

The individual executives had a good grasp of their view of risk, but they had never discussed it as a management team. While there were a lot of well-formed opinions, there was not a consolidated view and therefore no action plan. Without a consolidated view, the company could not define the costs and risk/reward of investing in protective measures. They could not develop a risk management plan.

Step One: Define, Rate, And Rank Company Risks

For this company, the first step was to separate insurable from uninsurable risks. The insurable risks had been handled consistently and responsibly by the CFO. The board reviewed the program and agreed most of it was appropriate but wanted to spend more time understanding cyber coverage. Since this is a rapidly evolving area, this effort was needed.

The harder part was to define, rate, and rank the intangible risks to the business. This is a classic case of the value being in the process; considerable debate and head-scratching were needed to produce a simplistic looking outcome.

Over a series of board meetings, with committee meetings in between, the directors debated the risks across the enterprise as well as within individual lines of business. A simple rating system was used to force rank issues. As this rolled up, it represented the accumulated thoughts and opinions of all of the directors.

Step Two: Continue Managing Business Risks Each Quarter

Establishing a risk management plan is not enough. It must be continuously managed. The second step is the ongoing monitoring and course corrections needed to keep the risk management system current.

Each quarter, the board takes a deeper dive into one or two specific issues. Over the course of a year, each major risk is thoroughly vetted. Budgets can be set and adjusted based on changing conditions and risk tolerance.

Preparing For The Unexpected: Part Of The Board's Duty Of Care

Family and other private businesses still have a fiduciary duty to their shareholders, whether they are key executives or minor children. The duty of care is a prime responsibility for all fiduciary directors, regardless of ownership structure. Managing business risks is the essence of duty of care for directors.

Make sure you and your directors establish a risk management plan that addresses all the potential risks and threats to your business. If you are diligent about the process, your company will be protected for years to come.

Let's examine what goes into creating a system to manage risk.

Developing A Risk Management System

Large organizations use ISO standards to develop policies and procedures because market forces and internal challenges demand standardization.

ISO 31000 is where large companies are likely to start developing their risk management system, but private companies often benefit from a more practical approach.

Developing a risk management system for a business is a process, not an event. Typically, the greatest value is from doing the work, not the final outcome. The process of thinking through "what can go wrong?" and "how bad can it be?" to "what can I do about it?" is what informs management and the board of what they might be facing.

For private companies, the first discussion of risk management is often when a board is formed, and the outsiders start asking about it. If this happens, you need to design the process to develop the risk management system before you start the work.

If that is your situation, consider these questions as a starting point:

How will you separate the insurable from the uninsurable risks? Everyone understands insurance. The insurable risks are usually handled by the CFO, with an annual review. If there is a question of coverage and deductibles, they may need to go to the board for review. As the insurance industry innovates, it offers new products to cover risks that were previously not covered, e.g., reps and warranty or cyber coverages.

What types of risks should we focus on? Think about events that may cause a debt default, bankruptcy, major loss of talent, or brand damage. A 10 percent drop in revenue is ordinary business. You still need to deal with routine risks, but this conversation is to identify, quantify, and potentially mitigate events that are so large you would not prepare for them in the ordinary course of business.

Who should be included? Who on the management team can materially contribute to the thought process? The three parts of the process are (1) identifying risks, (2) evaluating the impact, and (3) considering mitigation strategies. You are looking for creative thinkers who can see what is not obvious and won't rush to evaluate ideas too early.

Is this a group or individual activity? Some people do better by starting this as a solo activity and then comparing notes. Others need group interaction to spur thought. Since there are no right answers, think about your corporate culture and the scenarios where you get the best cross-functional results.

Should people work outside their area of responsibility? Functional leaders are likely quick to make a list of what they are worried about. There are natural frictions within a management team, e.g., sales versus production. What are the benefits of having leaders examine each other's areas? Does it provide more insight, or does it trigger challenged relationships? In some cases, this may serve as a good team-building exercise, and that may influence how you design the process.

How much time is this worth? By its nature, there is no natural end to this process, so it needs to be managed. The initial goal is to get a substantive working document that is exhaustive but also has the buy-in of the team. This should go to the board to reflect upon and provide feedback.

The first time through tends to be a bit arduous since you need to figure out "how to" do it in addition to doing the work. Practically, two or three rounds of development should produce a working document, and then maybe one more round before it goes to the board.

After that, the annual review should be an hour or two unless there has been a change in the business or a substantive change in the management team.

How does this fit the timing of annual activities? Budgeting, performance reviews, and strategic planning tend to have annual cycles driven by the fiscal year cycle. A risk management discussion is not tied to a specific time of the year. If you look at all the annual events of this type, find a blank spot in the calendar and think about discussing risk then.

Risk management is an ongoing activity that needs to be reviewed by the board in-depth, at least annually. The hardest part of developing a risk management system is often just getting started.

As noted previously, private and family businesses still have a fiduciary duty to their shareholders, even if they are spouses or minor children. The duty of care is a prime responsibility for all fiduciary directors, regardless of ownership structure. Managing risk is the essence of duty of care for directors.

ENTERPRISE RISK ASSESSMENT

	Enterprise Risk			
	Severity of Risk	Likelihood of Risk	Preparedness to Mitigate the Risk	Comments
Please rate each Enterprise Risk on Three Dimensions: • Severity of the risk • Likelihood of the risk • Preparedness to mitigate the risk	4. 3. 2. 1.	5. 4. 3. 2. 1.	3. 2. 1.	
Top Enterprise Risks — 1. Management Risks				
2. Competitive Risks				
3. Supplier Risks				
4. Regulatory Risks				
5. Technology Risks				
6. Environmental Risks				

Figure 10

Severity of Risk
4. May impact the long-term viability of the business
3. May significantly impact the margins of the business over the long term
2. May significantly impact the short-term financial health of the business
1. May impact the short-term financial health of the business

Likelihood of Risk
5. Extremely likely /Will happen
4. Very likely
3. Somewhat likely
2. Not very likely
1. Not likely at all

Preparedness to Mitigate the Risk
3. We do not understand this risk the way we should and need to devote more time and resources preparing
2. We need to improve our preparation for this risk and/or devote more resources to mitigating this risk
1. We understand and are prepared for this risk and should not devote more resources unless something changes

Help Avoid Buyer's Remorse With A Thorough Acquisition Risk Assessment

Sometimes what feels like a once-in-a-lifetime deal can be less lucrative than you thought after weighing the acquisition risks. Acquiring a company may increase customer base or cash flow but its labor dynamics or opportunities for new markets may not justify the risk of purchase, leading to potential buyer's remorse.

Take this example:

At a client's board meeting, we were evaluating making a bid on a rival business worth $100 million. Our management had spent years positioning itself for the opportunity to obtain this business, and now that acquisition was finally upon us. Even though it was an extremely large transaction for the buyer, the bank was prepared to provide financing, thanks to a strong relationship. The transaction would catapult this second-generation business into a higher league. The younger generation was itching for growth. It would be a defining moment for the business.

The natural growth rate of the industry is slightly less than gross domestic product (GDP). The industry is filled with cash cows but not many shooting stars. It is heavily regulated, and the regulations vary by state, so this was the only attractive target adjacent to the core market, which should allow for economies of scale by combining operations.

What We Found in the Acquisition Diligence Process

Our due diligence process revealed material differences in how we ran the same type of business. Labor utilization, management depth, and compensation methods were all contrasting. Their differences made for a much more profitable business. But we also knew the seller had a reputation for being a substandard place to work, and it was unclear what employment law risks they were taking to obtain better financial performance.

But a successful acquisition and integration would produce a dominant market force and significant cash flows for the owners. There would not be another opportunity like this in the buyer's core market, likely in their lifetime.

How Do We Pay for This? And Should We?

Everyone was enthusiastic about the opportunity until I raised the unexpected question: "What is the IRR, and how are we going to pay for it?"

The excitement of the opportunity, coupled with the fact that we could fund the acquisition, caused people to forget two basic but very important questions: How would we get our money back, plus a profit, for taking the risk? And how much profit was required to justify the risk? After all, an acquisition of this size effectively bets the company on a single decision, with no way to back out.

When evaluating how we'd get our money back, the acquisition risks became clear. Buying this company was really about buying cash flows and customers since there weren't many other ways to guarantee a return:

- It would not take the buyer into new products, new markets, or complementary industries.
- The target was already lean so there were limited cost reduction opportunities.
- The growth rates were nominal so we could not rely on growth to generate IRR.
- Financial engineering would help but the buyer did not want too much leverage since they had experienced severe downturns in the industry in the past.

With these challenges, how else do you pay for an acquisition?

The math just didn't work. Even though it would be a great business to own and the financing was available, the deal was underwater. It was a classic case of being a good business to own but a tough business to buy. Acquisitions can be exciting but that doesn't mean they should be executed. Sometimes choosing not to act is the right decision, though inaction may feel less satisfying in the moment.

Questions to Ask In Your Acquisition Risk Assessment

Even if your company has spent years weighing its options as to whether to acquire what your managers believe (and hope) to be a lucrative deal, there may still be questions to answer before purchasing. The bigger the price tag, scale, and complexity of a deal, the greater need for careful reflection. There may be contrasting methods where the management, compensation, and/or labor is concerned, and these contrasts are not to be taken lightly. Before signing on the dotted line, raise the questions:

- What is the IRR?
- How do we pay for it?
- How will we get our money back, plus risk?
- Is the risk too great?
- How much profit is necessary to justify the risk?

If the higher-ups in your company can agree the acquisition risks are worth it, and everyone draws the same conclusions from the complete data, then congratulations! You have yourself a brand new company. If not, you will most likely be glad you asked the questions you did, subsequently saving yourself a lot of money, time, and heartache. The dissatisfaction of choosing not to do a deal is a far better outcome than buyer's remorse.

Chapter 12 Takeaways

Board Function: Risk Management

Develop a risk management system. Make sure you and your directors establish a risk management plan that addresses all the potential risks and threats to your business. If you are diligent about the process, your company will be protected for years to come.

Understand that developing a risk management system is a process. Typically, the greatest value is from doing the work, more so than the final outcome. The process of thinking through "what can go wrong?" and "how bad can it be?" to "what can I do about it?" is what informs management and the board of what they might be facing.

Define, rate, and rank the uninsurable risks. The hard part is to define, rate, and rank the intangible risks to the business. Considerable debate and head-scratching are needed to produce a simplistic looking outcome.

Continue managing business risks each quarter. Establishing a risk management plan is not enough. It must be continuously managed. Ongoing monitoring and course corrections are needed to keep the risk management system current.

Take a deeper dive. Each quarter, the board should take a deeper dive into one or two specific issues. Over the course of a year, each major risk is thoroughly vetted. Budgets can be set and adjusted based on changing conditions and risk tolerance.

Prepare for the unexpected. Family and private company boards have a fiduciary duty to their shareholders even if they are spouses or minor children. The duty of care is a prime responsibility for all fiduciary directors, regardless of ownership structure. Managing business risks is the essence of the duty of care for directors.

Afterword

Board Evaluations

If the board evaluates the company, who should evaluate the board? Let me share a few concluding thoughts on feedback through evaluations.

As leadership author Ken Blanchard says, "Feedback is the breakfast of champions."

Blanchard advises business leaders to be grateful for what you hear, even if it hurts. Don't shoot the messenger, he says: "If you get defensive, it could poison the environment and undo all the good work you've done to create psychological safety and establish caring relationships."[21]

I prefer the words of Frank Sonnenberg, author of *Listen to Your Conscience: That's Why You Have One*: "Feedback turns good into better and better into best."

Constructive Feedback Improves Performance

We have all seen how constructive feedback improves performance and helps employees to avoid mistakes. The challenge is getting actionable feedback to people early enough for them to use it effectively. In a private company, designing effective board evaluations can be an efficient way to support healthy company growth.

This approach applies to the company's board of directors as well as employees. Board evaluations started as an academic research topic in the 1990s. In 2003, the NYSE required listed companies to conduct annual board appraisals. Since then, most public companies have some type of annual board evaluation. Over the last ten years, a small industry of board evaluation consultants has emerged. While they serve public and private companies, most of their revenue is derived from public companies.

Designing Fruitful Board Evaluations

As a broad generalization, the best practices of public companies trickle down to private companies slowly and selectively. While better private boards conduct regular evaluations, my observation is that most private boards have not matured to the point where they have a disciplined and consistent self-appraisal process. Designing board evaluations with intention will bring focus and purpose to the assessment process.

Structuring And Designing Board Evaluations That Succeed

Many private companies use a non-fiduciary board of advisors as the primary governance body so the fiduciary board becomes a subset of the board of advisors. Owners want to add the skills and experience they lack but only to the extent they desire. This is a natural step in the evolution of a private company's governance. It is also one of the benefits of private ownership: you can do what you want so long as you can afford it.

There are four key questions to address when considering a board evaluation.

What Is The Purpose Of The Evaluation?

Just because it is considered best practice does not mean it is right for every situation or one size fits all. The process should be geared for the specific needs of your organization.

A new board needs time to evolve to achieve full effectiveness, and feedback is a quick way to see where it needs to grow in regard to basic governance responsibilities. A mature board will likely want to dive deeper into assessing how well it deals with succession planning, capital allocation, and risk management, as well as keeping the board itself vibrant via term limits.

Who Is Contributing To The Evaluation?
As for management and staff, 360-degree reviews often give the best feedback. That means the board performance evaluation should include board members, key non-board executives, and ownership representation. This can be tricky, depending on how healthy the working relationship is.

Who Should Conduct The Evaluation?
Who is best qualified to handle this task? It usually falls to the chairperson, outside counsel, or a consultant. The facilitator must be trusted by all participants so they can get candid responses. The leader also needs to have the tact and gravitas to deliver feedback so it is accepted. This is why an outsider may have to be considered.

How Do You Best Conduct The Evaluation?
The two most popular methods are questionnaires and personal interviews. The design and use of each is critical, but there are ample tools available in the public domain to get a start. If this is something new for the organization, an informal approach may make it easier for people to be candid and fully engaged.

The cottage industry of consultants has well-developed tools for public companies. Private companies should consider a modification of these methods to meet their individual needs and budgets.

Are Private Companies Really Evaluating Their Boards?
There are a handful of qualified surveys of private company director compensation. There is little to no reviewed data on private companies' board evaluations.

Based on hearsay, I estimate that less than 15 percent of private company boards use a formal evaluation process on a routine basis. This is more a function of how long the board has been functioning rather than the size of the company.

However, there always seems to be time to do this on an ad hoc basis after a crisis, e.g., death/resignation of a director, global pandemic, management shakeup. This is consistent with the maxim that owners are good at working *in* the business but most are not as good at working *on* the business.

The decision to conduct an evaluation and how it is used is really a measure of the quality of the ownership of the business. Good owners will drive continuous improvement at all levels of the business, including the board. They want to know the IRR of their investment in the board as much as they would any other investment.

Based on data from PwC, which surveyed public company directors, the need for continuous feedback is a top concern for many directors. In 2019, 49 percent of listed company directors stated that at least one director on their board should be replaced due to underperformance—though the ability to provide honest and anonymous feedback is also lacking for many directors. With only 44 percent of S&P 500 boards using some form of individual director assessment, it's clear even fewer private companies are catching these performance problems cited by director surveys.[22]

Prioritizing Evaluations As A Business Owner And A Director

All of the tools and personnel for conducting a board evaluation are readily available; it is a matter of priority. How important is designing board evaluations to the owners? Since there is no preset protocol, the process can be sized to budget constraints. Just because it may be sensitive, awkward, or a confidential matter does not mean it should not be dealt with proactively. The board is managing the most important business of the firm; it needs to be held accountable.

As an outside director, this should be an important part of your diligence process when considering joining a board. If there is no board evaluation process, why not? Has the board not evolved to that point yet, are the owners unwilling to invest in designing board evaluations, or is this an issue for a new director to lead on?

The board also gives its share of feedback to the business. Let's consider how that feedback can lead to necessary change.

Agents of Change: The Advantages Of Non-Executive Directors

Whether a company is public or private, the mission of its board of directors is to provide leadership in oversight, strategy, capital structure, succession planning, and risk management. While regulators will enforce matters at public companies, non-executive directors are often the only external force to drive change at private companies.

So long as the bank is happy and the taxes are paid, private and family business owners can drift off course for quite a while. Effective outside directors need to be the "adult in the room" to keep the business healthy and the insiders focused on the best interests of the business.

Effective Non-Executive Directors Start With Accountability

Aside from providing broader business experience and corporate governance duties, company and advisor firms cite "checks and balances" as one of the main advantages of non-executive directors, according to the QCA 2020 Non-Executive Director Survey.[23]

Holding management accountable is one of a board's highest obligations and one of the greatest advantages of non-executive directors. Here are three examples that will test the leadership within a business. In each scenario, you can see there is trouble ahead:

- A family executive lacks the talent and passion needed to run the business.
- A tenured, loyal employee has risen to a senior position well above their competency.
- The industry has been disrupted by technology or foreign competition, and the company is unable to respond.

The solutions don't come from spreadsheets or a new app. They come from determined individuals standing up to work through the issue. In these examples, the outsiders need to be the change agents.

The Dysfunction Of Division

My observation is that dysfunctional firms tend to segregate into two types: battlegrounds and libraries. At the former, constant conflicts within management motivate non-combatants to duck and cover as much as possible. Other firms are like libraries: no one talks about the issues, preferring a quiet, false façade rather than addressing the conflict.

Neither is effective. Healthy companies detect trouble early and deal with it directly.

Characteristics Of Effective Independent Directors

If you are a non-executive director at a private company, most likely you are there to make sure these situations get dealt with constructively.

To be successful at these matters, outside directors who bring positive results need to hold three convictions:

- Bad news does not get better with time.
- Work the business issue and avoid the personality flaws.
- You were elected to lead on the tough issues. Now is the time to perform.

In a recent situation, our board was dealing with a long-standing CEO who did not have the skills and personality to lead the business through a season of disruptive change. While a valued employee and close friend of the non-executive owner, he was the wrong person to take the business forward. Separating the CEO meant rupturing a fifteen-year friendship.

As the lead outside director, I was responsible for driving the process through evaluation, decision-making, separation, and the eventual transition process. The trick was getting the owner to put aside his personal loyalties and focus on the needs of the business analysis.

After a tense board meeting, the decision was finally made to separate the CEO; there was no other option given the details of the situation. The CEO needed to hear this from the owner to know there was no room for negotiation. The owner was a technologist, not a businessperson. After much introspection, the owner realized he didn't know how to get through this without letting his emotions interfere.

External Directors Recognize When Third-Party Counsel Is Needed

When the owner asked me, "How should I handle this?" I realized to fulfill my duty as the lead external director, I needed to step into the situation even deeper. With counsel, we prepared the owner for each of the likely scenarios that might arise during the termination process. I told the owner to expect to feel uncomfortable; this is not supposed to be easy. I counseled him to be respectful, direct, and stay focused on the business issues, not the personalities.

The CEO's mismanagement also meant there was little cash available to fund a severance package. A reasonable offer was made but the CEO pushed back, threatening multiple lawsuits for discrimination and nuisance claims. After toning down the rhetoric and asking a few pointed questions, we understood what was important to him. So we traded away a few restrictive covenants to avoid giving away cash and quickly achieved closure.

Outside directors are often the only force that can break a stalemate and provide leadership to take a private company through a perilous situation. This is one of the key reasons why private companies should seek competent and effective non-executive directors—to provide strong leadership when companies need it most.

How To Assist Board Members With Signs Of Dementia

One reason board work is attractive to aging professionals is that for private companies there is typically no mandatory retirement age. While there are likely to be term limits, as there should be, one can perform board work as long as they serve the needs of the organization. It is not as physically taxing as full-time executive work. Many people pursue board work since it provides significant professional engagement while still allowing them to "slow down" and enjoy life a little more.

So what happens when a director may start to mentally decline while still having a fiduciary duty to the corporation?

None of us are immune to the risks of mental decline or dementia as we age. Some forms of dementia start as early as your thirties and forties, although the dominant forms start after age sixty-five or so.

Dementia means the impairment of memory, thinking, and/or a decline in social skills. Here are some indications of dementia:

- Cognitive: mental decline, confusion in the evening hours, disorientation, inability to speak or understand language, making things up, mental confusion, or inability to recognize common things
- Behavioral: irritability, personality changes, restlessness, lack of restraint, or wandering and getting lost
- Mood: anxiety, loneliness, mood swings, or nervousness
- Psychological: depression, hallucinations, or paranoia
- Muscular: inability to combine muscle movements or unsteady walking
- Also common: memory loss, falling, jumbled speech, or sleep disorder

This is a multi-faceted issue. There are concerns for their well-being. Additionally, there are concerns about the decisions this person is making. Their decline will impact relationships within the organization and their family. One must also consider whether this person holds relationships with customers or suppliers that impact the organization, and how that will affect the person and the company.

When should someone intercede, and how best to handle it?

Determining A Course Of Action And Handling The Situation With Care And Respect

There is a body of law, elder law, which addresses the legalities of decision-making capacity, and when society should step in to make decisions for someone whose thinking may be impaired. If you have an issue, you should get trusted counsel to understand how the law impacts your choices.

But as emphasized by James Toomey, a lecturer on law at Harvard Law School who specializes on elder law, good counsel in this context is not just about having the best and smartest lawyers. These delicate, deeply personal situations are best handled by lawyers who have a relationship with the affected individual and the business. They need to have a deep sense of who the individual is and how they see themselves in older age. Elder law works best as an ongoing relationship, not a one-off transaction.

From a governance perspective, here are some of the questions to consider:

Where is the evidence of impairment? A poor decision is not the same as an impaired decision. Disagreeing with a decision is not a reason to judge capabilities. Dementia may demonstrate itself in many ways. There are specific tests to assess a person who may be showing signs of dementia or impaired decision-making. Directors can suggest this be looked at but need to be thoughtful about when and to whom this question is asked. This is more complicated in family businesses, of course.

Who is affected? Is this person an employee of the firm? An independent director? A family member? What social relationships do they have that will influence how to proceed? How do we keep control of the issue and give the person the best support?

Who has the right, or responsibility to intercede? There are no good rules on this, except the rules of common sense. How would you want to be treated if you were in this position?

How do you protect their dignity? Dignity often becomes the guiding factor when dealing with mental impairment. Your character will be assessed by the organization and the community based on how you handle the situation.

Societies are often measured by how they treat their least fortunate members, especially when those individuals can't speak or advocate for themselves.

How do you keep this out of court? If at all possible, it is best to keep these matters out of the legal system. Going to court makes everything more complicated. The bylaws should have a mechanism to remove a director for cause. Term limits are another way to deal with this. The risk is that an employee or an owner is in question. Their rights as an owner should not be impinged. But if their decision authority is due to ownership, things get blurry.

Therefore, follow these two steps:

Get advice from multiple viewpoints. In these situations, you will likely benefit from getting advice from more than one point of view. The answers are likely obtuse. With most of these disease processes, there is time to construct and evaluate a decision tree. Use that time wisely.

Organize the team. This is a perfect case of why relationships matter. Getting the best answers in these situations is often a team effort.

Dealing with dementia, in a business context, is likely to be a trial-and-error process. You should expect to make mistakes but avoid making big ones by having empathy for the affected individual and working closely with your team. To a large extent, how you communicate is equally if not more important than what you communicate.

And In Closing

Governance is like a bespoke suit—custom fit for only one person. What works best for one company may not be just right for the next company.

While it is valuable to ask others how their board works, I encourage you to experiment to find what is just right for your business.

If you are a board candidate, this book also has something just for you. Appendix B has advice on how to prepare for your search, how to perform due diligence on new opportunities, and what market forces you will face.

If you are a business owner, each chapter of this book has a lesson on how to push your board to do more for your business. Some will be more pertinent to your situation than others, and that is to be expected. If you take away just one or two important learnings from this book, I will consider it a success.

Afterword | 161

I hope you find this book useful. Please let me know what you think by sending an email to Bruce@KonaAdvisors.com.

Afterword Takeaways
Board Evaluations

Understand what governance is. Governance is like a bespoke suit—custom fit for only one person. What works best for one company may not be just right for the next company. While it is valuable to ask others how their boards work, I encourage you to experiment to find what is just right for your business.

Determine the advantages of outside directors. Whether a company is public or private, the mission of its board of directors is to provide leadership in oversight, strategy, capital structure, succession planning, and risk management. While regulators will enforce matters at public companies, outside directors are often the only external force to drive change at private companies.

Realize the need to hold management accountable. Holding management accountable is one of a board's highest obligations and one of the greatest advantages of having outside directors.

Know when to rely on external directors to recognize when third-party counsel is needed. Outside directors are often the only force that can break a stalemate and provide leadership to take a private company through a perilous situation. This is one of the key reasons why private companies should seek non-executive directors—to provide strong leadership when companies need it most.

Be aware that constructive feedback improves performance. Better private boards conduct regular evaluations, but most private company boards do not regularly evaluate their own performance. The decision to conduct an evaluation is really a measure of the quality of the ownership of the business.

Appendix

A – Chapter Takeaways

B – Advice for Candidates

C – Acknowledgments

D – About the Author

E – Index

F – Works Referenced And Author's Notes

Appendix

Appendix A – **Chapter Takeaways**

Chapter 1 Takeaways

The Ownership Journey And Governance

Your ownership strategy should drive your business strategy. Develop a statement of life goals and decide how the business must perform so you can achieve them.

Manage capital and talent to drive the business strategy. All businesses need capital and talent to succeed. Private businesses tend to be constrained in both.

Think about your governance needs. While the focus needs to be on growing value, risk management cannot be ignored. What governance structures are needed to provide oversight and perspective along the way?

Plan for management succession. Continuity of management is considered the biggest risk in business. It must be managed successfully to ensure the continuity of the business.

Manage the exit process thoughtfully. Building a great business often seems like the hard part, but it is really the preamble. A successful exit of choice is the capstone of a great career.

Know how to maintain focus, demonstrate tenacity, and practice adaptability. Priorities matter because time, talent, and resources are scarce and need to be allocated to their highest and best use. When you see your situation change, assess the change, and adapt to the new reality quickly.

Manage expectations. When you combine focus, adaptability, and a practical understanding of what your organization can achieve, allow yourself to manage your own expectations.

Ask for help. Don't be afraid to ask for help when you need it. This can be tough when you are firefighting, whether due to a lack of resources or just having a tough go of it.

Hold yourself accountable. This is often the hardest task of all. Very few people do this well consistently, year in and year out for decades.

Chapter 2 Takeaways

What Is Private Company Governance And Why Does It Matter?

Seek wisdom. Board work should provide wisdom to solve long-term issues, which is best done through active discussion. Boards are responsible for oversight, strategy, capital structure, management succession, and risk management.

Determine board size. While public companies often have tens of directors, I've found private companies usually do best with five to seven people in the room.

Foster independence. For private companies, good advice and accountability are needed. The outside directors need enough independence to maintain clear judgment.

Assign committee work. Most private company boards do not have separate committees, although larger ones do. Managing audits and compensation requires experience beyond general management.

Name a strong chair. Public companies may wrestle with whether the CEO should be chair or if the duties should be split. Private companies typically don't have this quandary, but they need to have a strong chair.

Evaluate board compensation. This is always a delicate subject, but it is not without ample data to use for input.

Chapter 3 Takeaways

Defining The Goals Of Your Board

Define the board's mandate. A board charter is different from an entity's bylaws or operating agreement. The charter explains the reason the board exists, what it is expected to accomplish, and how it should function.

Choose the right board style. In addition to the needs of the business, the board becomes a reflection of the owners' needs and personalities.

Consider the costs/benefits. Because bringing in outside directors is a sensitive topic for some, it is worthwhile to understand the costs, benefits, and ROI before making the commitment. The typical concerns are money, time, interpersonal dynamics, and potential interference with the business and ownership.

Choose the right board type. There are three types of advisory boards: consulting, junior, and full advisory boards. They represent a scaling up of board capabilities to match the owners' and business's needs.

Build a high-performing board. Achieving a high-performing board with outside directors in a private company is not a simple matter. It requires a thoughtful needs assessment, a carefully crafted board mandate, meticulous recruiting and onboarding, and an unrelenting focus on director and board performance.

Chapter 4 Takeaways

Recruiting And Retaining Directors And Advisors

Realize that establishing a board is a process, not an event. Getting to the first meeting may require six to nine months or longer. This time is used to draft a charter; define candidate qualifications; build a pool of competitive candidates; run the interview process; select and then onboard the candidates.

Think long-term. Getting the new board to become a cohesive decision-making body typically requires a year of operation. If they only spend four days a year working together, that is not much time to get to know one another and develop trust. Active committees do help in this regard.

Understand the constituencies. The board's mandate and its members need to be focused on the needs of their constituencies. While this is generally understood as ownership, the word "stakeholder" is commonly used for good reasons.

Deliver a clear mandate. You should form a board to advise the ownership on critical questions. These few questions should anticipate the major issues that are likely to occur during the next three to five years.

Manage the players. Don't be afraid to change players in the middle of the game. Sometimes a candidate presents and interviews well but doesn't fit in with everyone else.

Include the management team. The top tier of management that is not on the board may provide critical support for the board's deliberations. It helps to have these functional leaders present to the board on a rotating basis.

Chapter 5 Takeaways
Costs Of A Board And Compensation

Focus on strategy. A high-performing board helps management formulate and execute a strategy to achieve the owner's objectives. This often drives the ROI of the board. Many private businesses lack this kind of formal planning process.

Outside directors bring a great deal. Outside directors can bring a systematic approach to developing business strategy, allocating resources, and providing accountability. Outsiders may bring relationships to help deploy the strategy.

For companies under $20 million. Private companies under $20 million in revenue tend not to have boards, and if they do, they are informal advisory boards. There tends to be little compensation, as these are "golf buddies" and not traditional, independent outside directors.

For companies in the $20 million–$50 million range. These businesses are starting to form advisory boards with a semblance of normalized function, although many are "consulting boards" and not yet advisory boards. Compensation here tends to be a day rate for professional time.

For companies in the $50 million–$200 million range. These boards tend to be true advisory boards, with regular schedules, agendas, and meaningful structure. Compensation is typically in the $20,000 to $30,000 per year range and may be structured several different ways.

For companies above $200 million. Compensation increases to the $25,000 to $75,000 per year range, with a wider variation in structure and total compensation. Many of these boards are fiduciary.

Feedback can cause discomfort. It is true for boards as well as for people. Thoughtful board evaluations are the best way to achieve a high ROI from a board. An evaluation may be performed on the board as a unit and/or individual board members. There are numerous techniques to accomplish this delicate task.

Chapter 6 Takeaways

Planning Effective Board Meetings

A board is outside the chain of command. A board is designed to push back and hold accountable the forces of authority. Employees are expected to follow the directions they are given. Boards are designed to question those directions to generate better outcomes.

An effective board meeting agenda requires planning. Most people don't think about how a board meeting agenda is created or about what goes into it. But planning ahead is a vital element in having an effective board and productive board meetings. This is the chairperson's responsibility.

Minimize reporting, maximize discussion, and improve decision-making time. Board time is precious. It should not be wasted on reporting that can be done through pre-reads and ancillary conversations. Deliver the board book far enough in advance so participants can read it, consider it, and prepare questions.

Maintain an annual cycle of evergreen topics. Certain subjects need to be addressed every year, and it is beneficial to spread them out over twelve months to make meetings more manageable. Examples include strategy development, budgets, succession planning, performance evaluations, compensation, and risk management.

Make time for self-evaluation. Effective agendas reserve time for the board to evaluate itself. Board evaluations are complex and essential to board performance; it's important to include this time on the agenda at least annually.

Chapter 7 Takeaways

Role Of Committees: Audit, Compensation, and Nominating

Know that boards mature over time. The need for and effectiveness of committees will evolve as the board matures.

Be aware that a great audit process has no surprises. An audit needs to be done. But it should give owners comfort that their assets are being managed properly, and appropriate safeguards are in place.

Conduct management performance reviews. My experience suggests boards can improve performance reviews by asking these questions: How has the individual's performance driven success to achieve strategic goals? Is the individual a good fit for the role they are in, both today and in the future? How does the individual exemplify the values and culture we aspire to demonstrate?

Use boards to reduce risk. Boards are a powerful tool for creating value for owners and reducing the risks of ownership. But learning how to use them requires time and attention. Good owners understand this and invest the time to get more from their boards.

Keep your board fresh. Many private company boards do not have committees, and the chair is the owner, who is not skilled in this area. The lack of a nominating committee may cause the board to become stale. The outside directors are not going to push this issue until it is unavoidable.

Reassess near-term challenges. What issues does the board need to address over the next three to five years? Are the current members well-suited to those challenges? They may have been the right people for the past problems, but new problems suggest new talent is needed.

Evaluate and refine your expectations. Do you know what you want your board to accomplish? Is it an expectations issue or a communications issue that is causing discomfort or underachievement?

Chapter 8 Takeaways

Board Function: Oversight

Understand what board oversight is. The phrase "noses in, fingers out, sensors on" describes the mindset of a good director.

Understand complexity. There is no easy way to measure complexity or an increase in complexity. The most likely signs of change are step functions that create span of control, capital, and operational challenges.

Focus on scalability and complexity. Understand your ability to manage change. Change is hard. How adaptable is your organization? What might you need to do to get your staff ready for what is ahead of them?

Know that boards should anticipate future problems. Great partnerships are based on aligned interests and accepted rules for managing conflict. The bylaws or operating agreement of an entity codify how the most important decisions get made and who gets to make them.

Keep your organizational documents current. You should review your bylaws or operating agreement every three to five years to make sure they are current with your situation. These documents should be reviewed well in advance of a capital event.

Realize that boards reduce risks. Your board members should have accumulated enough battle scars to say, "Here's what we have learned in the past. Here's what you need to think about now and into the future." At the end of the day, you want your company's board to be filled with people you know who will be able to handle the unknown because they've done it before.

Chapter 9 Takeaways

Board Function: Strategy Development And Execution

Understand strategy development and execution is a process, not an event. Someone needs to manage the overall process since everyone already has a full-time job. That may be the most important decision of all when it comes to strategy.

Realize strategy needs to be consistent with the company's culture and persona. Organizations don't usually tolerate decisions that conflict with their inherent values. You know who you are, for better or worse. Don't fight your own DNA.

Know what the management team can actually get done. Once you figure out what needs to get done, be realistic about what can be done. If you lack the talent or bandwidth, figure that out first before launching a campaign that is destined to go nowhere.

Boards should hold management accountable. Ownership should give a clear mandate to the board on what it expects from the business. Traditionally, management develops a strategy to be reviewed and approved by the board. Then the board holds management accountable for delivering the approved plan. If these bodies are the same few people, who ensures accountability? For smaller organizations, this can be a difficult issue to grapple with.

Keep the plan current. PowerPoint reports have a short half-life. A strategy manifesto should be a living document; it should evolve over time as conditions change. An annual review is always appropriate, but be sure to stay in sync with the rate of change in your industry.

Chapter 10 Takeaways

Board Function: Management Succession Planning

Identify your management succession needs. One of the primary responsibilities of a board is to provide management continuity. Emergencies tend to resolve themselves since decisions can't wait. Proactive succession planning is the hallmark of a well-run organization.

Go all-in with the planning process. It starts with having a clear business strategy that drives your future leadership needs. Start with the answer and work backward. Succession planning is both a process and a project to be managed.

Know your timing. There is likely an immovable deadline to meet, such as a retirement. Give yourself enough time to figure it out.

Realize that thoughtful, timely communications are key. Who needs to know what, when, and why? Sometimes, what you don't say may be as important as what you do say.

Provide a clear mandate to the new CEO. The ownership group needs to be clear on what it wants this person to accomplish and when. The new CEO will value their time and be ambitious. They will likely want to accomplish something meaningful and not waste their time.

Have a transition timeline. The outgoing CEO needs to consider how they will turn over the reins to their successor. What can be achieved during onboarding? What takes more time? What do you "just have to be there" to understand? Key relationships with customers and suppliers take time. At what point in these relationships does the outgoing CEO stand in front of the new CEO, beside the new CEO, or behind them, and at what point do they walk away?

Let them do their job. After developing the transition plan, stick to it. The exiting CEO should disappear for a while—go to Hawaii for a month or something similar—to prove to the organization that the new CEO is really in charge.

Chapter 11 Takeaways

Board Function: Capital Structure

Focus on raising capital. Boards are responsible for oversight, strategy, management succession, capital structure, and risk management. Most of their time tends to focus on strategy and management. Once a business strategy is developed, it is then about finding the capital to fund growth and securing the talent to execute the plan.

Understand the market. You need to understand what the capital markets have to offer and what your business offers to them. Each potential investor has different expectations for IRR, yield, risk, and governance requirements. Take some time to understand these differences and why they are so. You need to understand their motivations and constraints before soliciting interest.

Plan far enough ahead. Raising capital typically becomes a six- to twelve-month process. You need to plan ahead in case the market decides to close just before you plan to enter it.

Board members should help to make introductions to intermediaries and capital sources. They should help with diligence and determining which professionals to engage. Board members should be the anchors for disciplining the process, protecting shareholders' interests, and managing conflicts between parties.

Consider you might just need a good lawyer. For some private companies, raising capital means securing a term loan or line of credit from a local bank. Sometimes it means selling a small piece of the business to a trusted friend or relative. Those types of transactions likely just need a good lawyer to get a deal done.

Chapter 12 Takeaways

Board Function: Risk Management

Develop a risk management system. Make sure you and your directors establish a risk management plan that addresses all the potential risks and threats to your business. If you are diligent about the process, your company will be protected for years to come.

Understand that developing a risk management system is a process. Typically, the greatest value is from doing the work, more so than the final outcome. The process of thinking through "what can go wrong?" and "how bad can it be?" to "what can I do about it?" is what informs management and the board of what they might be facing.

Define, rate, and rank the uninsurable risks. The hard part is to define, rate, and rank the intangible risks to the business. Considerable debate and head-scratching are needed to produce a simplistic looking outcome.

Continue managing business risks each quarter. Establishing a risk management plan is not enough. It must be continuously managed. Ongoing monitoring and course corrections are needed to keep the risk management system current.

Take a deeper dive. Each quarter, the board should take a deeper dive into one or two specific issues. Over the course of a year, each major risk is thoroughly vetted. Budgets can be set and adjusted based on changing conditions and risk tolerance.

Prepare for the unexpected. Family and private company boards have a fiduciary duty to their shareholders even if they are spouses or minor children. The duty of care is a prime responsibility for all fiduciary directors, regardless of ownership structure. Managing business risks is the essence of the duty of care for directors.

Appendix B – **Advice For Candidates**

This book is being written to help business owners achieve a more effective state of corporate governance. But it will also be read by people looking for their first board seat, and owners looking to start their first board. This appendix provides more context for first-time board members.

Board Diligence And Information Requests

Candidates should request the following information when they are evaluating a new board seat:

- Indemnification letter or bylaws indemnification
- D&O policy
- Minutes of board meetings—prior three years
- Bylaws; when were they most recently updated?
- Statutory guidelines on director liability for their domicile
- Insurance summaries
  - D&O—copy of full policy (A=individual, B=company, C=entity & board)
    - Defense costs to be outside policy limits
    - D&O application each year to see what potential issues may lead to a claim and therefore determine if there is a failure to disclose
    - M&A coverages, tax indemnity, contingent liability insurance
  - EPLI summary
  - Product liability
  - Product recall
  - Cyber
  - Industry-specific specialty coverages

- History of
  - Claims, settlements, and lawsuits
  - Dividends, payouts, any non-salary compensation to execs or outside family
- Any discussions of buy/sell with any shareholders, and what is their expectation?
  - Special directives from owners
- Audit committee reports
- History of communications to outside and family shareholders
- Management
  - Any recent turmoil, succession plans
  - Org chart
  - Executive performance appraisal systems
  - Expectations of non-family senior staff (compensation, succession)
- Union/labor history
- Strategic plan, if available
- Three-year audited financial statements
- Proforma forward budget
- Compliance manual
- HR policy manual
- Contact list of professionals: attorneys, bankers, accountants, auditors, consultants

Advice For Securing Your First Board Seat

Author's Note: Special thanks to Verna E. Lynch for her help in preparing this material.

With millions of private companies in the U.S. and a robust economy, it may seem that securing a board seat on a private company board should be less difficult than it was in the past. However, with increasing competition for board seats and the emphasis on diversity, board positions are more competitive than ever before.

Assumptions You've Made About Boards And Guidance For Obtaining A Board Seat

Most private companies under $100 million in revenue don't typically have a functioning fiduciary board since their governance needs have not evolved such that they can't function without it. They do tend to think about an advisory board as they grow through $25 million to $30 million in revenue since their challenges require perspective and/or experience the owners typically don't have themselves.

For companies with boards, there are typically only three seats assigned to outsiders. There tends to be little turnover due to how terms are structured, and the rate of retirement is minimal.

The supply of qualified candidates is multiples larger than the number of open seats at any time. If you think about how many people annually transition from full-time employment to board work or start to "slow down" a bit, the imbalance is clear.

Over the last five years, I have been involved in coaching hundreds of people on the board search process. For the typical candidate, here is where the conversation usually starts:

- Finding your first board seat is likely to take years, not months. There is no assurance it will ever happen either.
- For any open board seat, the search committee receives anywhere from one hundred to five hundred resumes, meaning you may not hear back from the organizations conducting the search. Given these numbers, regardless of your qualifications or level of effort, your chance of success is less than 1 percent at best.
- Gaining a board seat is more difficult than securing an executive role in an organization. The most effective way to improve your chances of securing a board seat is through relationships. The operative phrase is "it's who knows you, not who you know." You still need to do all the things cited below, but who knows you and will recommend you is the board equivalent of driving in the express lane.

- Many board members advise that the more direct you are in soliciting for an open seat, the less successful you may be. The best way to show you may be board material is to demonstrate judgment and tact while selling yourself at the same time.
- Be cautious with pre-paid board search organizations; caveat emptor.

Measures To Take For Securing A Board Seat

Well-functioning boards are carefully constructed to have the right combination of industry and functional expertise, governance experience, and other talents demanded by the situation. Each board is unique to the business it serves.

For newer boards in particular, a board matrix will identify candidates by the seat they are competing to fill, e.g., industry expertise, marketing expertise.

Before conducting outreach, prepare your resume, bio, and other materials to clearly differentiate yourself from others in the intense competition for board seats. Be ready to clearly communicate what you bring to the situation, why it is unique and valuable to the firm, and why you want to be on this board. Your communications should focus on:

- Industry expertise—identify the few key industries in which you have demonstrated expertise
- Functional expertise—pinpoint your areas of functional expertise sought by boards
- Unique skills– if you don't check the box for industry or functional expertise, note what you bring that moves their needle
- Personal attributes—note what sets you apart from a personality and character perspective

Start your marketing by reaching out to people you know and who are likely to know where the open seats may be, whether today or the near term. Remember, you are likely to need to nurse these relationships for years before they bear fruit. These people know you the best and are best suited for keeping you "top of mind" when they encounter board opportunities.

- Maintain or revitalize your network. Ask yourself who in my network is in the flow of board seat opportunities? These people will become your high priority networking opportunities.
- Reach out to these people to rekindle past conversations. Let them know what you're doing in your career, indicate your interest in developing yourself for board service, and highlight why you'd be a great board member.

How To Start Revitalizing Your Network

You should consider building a database of specific companies for which you might be a good fit as a board member; then start the relationship building.

- Once you have a list of names, dig deeper to understand their situation. Review public filings, trade magazines, and press releases as a starting point.
- Identify their directors, advisors, attorneys, CPAs, and consultants. Use LinkedIn to see if someone in your network can make a warm introduction.
- Before reaching out, research the individual. What are their interests and associations as defined in LinkedIn? There may be interests or associations you share that can facilitate relationship building.
- A direct introduction from someone in your network to the board member of interest is an effective way to start a dialog.
- The objective for this outreach is to build relationships and receive useful advice on the board search process. It is considered impolite to directly ask about a board opening unless your relationship is strong enough to have earned that privilege. Board members place their organization's interests first and they will not readily recommend someone they do not know, like, and trust.
- Ask for advice about something meaningful such as best practices for preparing for board service. For any relationship you are trying to build, you likely have two "portfolios" to discuss as you get acquainted:

1. The current role you play in your career narrative
2. The independent director role for which you are preparing
- Genuineness and patience are vitally important. Your efforts and dialog should be focused on building a sound business relationship, not narrowly focused on securing an unfair advantage in the interview process.

Leverage or build new networks with people who hear about board opportunities:

- Many people recommend building relationships with PE firms, which will have an interest in you if you have industry-recognized expertise or you can be pivotal in helping them to exit their investment. You should already know if you fit that description. PE firms tend to be industry-specific in their board recruiting processes.
- Dedicate some of your effort to turnaround shops, corporate attorneys, estate attorneys, valuation firms, managing partners of CPA firms, and investment bankers. These are the individuals who regularly interface with the people making decisions about board seats.
- Join and participate in board organizations, like PDA and NACD, and industry associations that reflect your expertise.

Additional Ways To Build Your Portfolio To Highlight Your Skill Set

Serving on non-profit boards is a logical step that accentuates your interest in serving on boards and learning about board governance. It will also provide valuable experience at the committee level. This is an obvious way to distinguish yourself from other candidates.

You should continue to develop your reputation as a thought leader. This demonstrates your functional and industry expertise and strengthens your personal brand. Be sure to use all relevant channels of social media to reach the people who can refer you to an opening. Use a tone of voice and demeanor that represents how a strong board candidate should present themselves.

Numerous retained search firms have reputable board practices. Try to identify firms that specialize in your area of focus. Otherwise, you may be wasting your time. Typically, these firms have an intake process on their websites. If you choose to reach out to these firms for networking, be aware they may not respond, considering the volume of inquiries they receive for a limited number of board seats.

Securing a board role is ultimately about personality and fit, and only through a genuine relationship can someone learn those attributes about you.

Practical Feedback For Active Directors

Author's Note: Special thanks to Stephanie Olexa, PhD, MBA for her help in preparing this material.

There is an increasing supply of qualified candidates looking for their first board seat with a private company. Experienced directors understand how the process works and what to expect. First-time candidates, however, are thirsty to learn how the process works and how best to get into the game.

There are considerable resources for candidates to understand the preparation and selection processes: trade associations, executive education programs, consultants, conferences, books, and webinars. Knowing where to start is in itself a likely challenge.

Our experience working with candidates, and having run numerous search processes, is that potential candidates seek advice in these four categories:

1. Understanding the motivations and benefits of service
2. Creating an individualized plan to prepare for the selection process
3. Learning how the selection process works
4. Getting feedback from active directors on how compensation evolves over time

Motivation

Before thinking about competing for a board seat, it is important to understand what the position is and isn't and be sure your motivations and interests align with the company's needs and expectations.

There are many reasons to seek a board seat. The distilled wisdom of experienced directors is consistent: don't do it for the money. While the compensation usually respects the director's time and contribution, for most candidates it does not provide enough motivation to accept the risk and responsibilities. You need a more powerful motivation.

When asked why they serve, experienced directors consistently say they serve to: (1) have an impact on the business; (2) stay engaged in the business community, typically as they move toward retirement; or (3) support a business they have an affinity for.

Many directors seek seats as a means to network for other personal reasons. One director has said one of the greatest benefits he has enjoyed are the friendships he has made with other directors. He cited that several of his fellow directors have become dear friends even though their mutual board work ended years ago.

Compensation

Candidates always wonder about compensation, so it is important to know the market. Public company, private equity, and venture capital companies are outside the data presented herein. These comments apply to private and family-owned businesses, typically in the $10 million to $300 million revenue range in the U.S.

The rule of thumb has long been that companies in this range pay from $20,000 to $40,000 per year, using retainers, meeting fees, and other forms of compensation. Some include equity, but less so with family-owned businesses. These figures trend higher as revenues exceed $300 million, but not significantly higher.

These figures are in the middle of the market and there are numerous exceptions. One company sets director compensation by determining the CEO's hourly rate and applying it to the number of hours per year expected from directors.

There have been several credible board compensation studies performed over the years, with the two well-known sources being the Private Company

Board Compensation and Governance studies from 2019 and 2021 and nine years of data from Lodestone Global.

The compensation should respect your time and commitment but should not be viewed as a primary means of financial security.

Education And Training

Success in the C-suite is not enough to be successful in the boardroom. Boardroom dynamics require a collegial style of intellectual engagement and rigor. Directors are bound by both a duty of care and a duty of loyalty. Directors have grave responsibilities but should not be making operating decisions or directing staff, other than interacting with direct reports to the board. The common phrase is "noses in, fingers out, sensors on."

Candidates with strong executive styles tend to be very directive in their behaviors—a command and control approach to interaction. Successful directors need to be active listeners and highly collaborative. Demonstrating this style shift from the former to the latter is a critical part of the interview process and candidates often fail to advance if they cannot quickly demonstrate their ability to behave as a good director should.

There is a cottage industry of established firms, consultants, conferences, and academic programs to prepare people to become directors. They vary in quality, focus, geographic reach, delivery method, and expense.

Having worked with or had conversations with many of them, the good news is that candidates have many options. It is also a situation where "caveat emptor" needs to be employed.

Candidates looking for help to prepare their written materials (board resume, bio, LinkedIn) can expect to pay $750 to $3,000 depending on who they choose to work with.

Academic programs vary from $1,500 to $10,000, proportionate to their duration (one day to one week) and brand identification; conferences typically cost up to $2,500 for a two- or three-day event. NACD runs several programs but these tend to target public companies and may not be the right fit for candidates only looking at private company seats.

The Private Directors Association offers a Certificate in Private Company Governance as its keystone educational offering.

The individual consultants in this market typically charge $5,000 to $10,000 for a suite of services that is likely to include resume writing, interview preparation, coaching, and some degree of search support.

The online databases where candidates pay a fee to receive opportunities also tend to provide resume writing and coaching services as a complement to their primary offerings.

There are several firms in the UK and Europe that focus on those geographies, offering similar services to their US counterparts.

Feedback From Experienced Directors

One comment we hear from experienced directors is that once compensation is set, it does not change much over time. The data supports this observation. We found these comments to be instructive:

- "Supply significantly outstrips demand. For example, in a recent search for a family business, they were looking for three directors for a new board, and we received almost eight hundred applications!"
- "Inertia is a huge force to contend with; once compensation is set, owners don't like to adjust it."
- "Owners question the value the board produces. The benefits are difficult to measure, but the expenses and time commitment is material."
- "They are not creating the value we had hoped, so why should I pay them more?"
- "There are ten people in line for each slot, so why increase the pay?"
- "I know they are using our board as a steppingstone to get on a public board, so why should I pay a lot?"

What tends to come as a surprise, but is consistent, is that the most overwhelmingly common value perceived by owners was some variation of,

"The board forced our management team to review their data every quarter and be prepared to give a presentation, so it increased our accountability."

It is often difficult for entrepreneurs and owners to hold themselves accountable, so they often need independent outsiders enforce accountability.

This ties back directly to the discussions of motivations. Overwhelmingly, experienced directors say, "Don't do it for the money, do it because you want to have an impact."

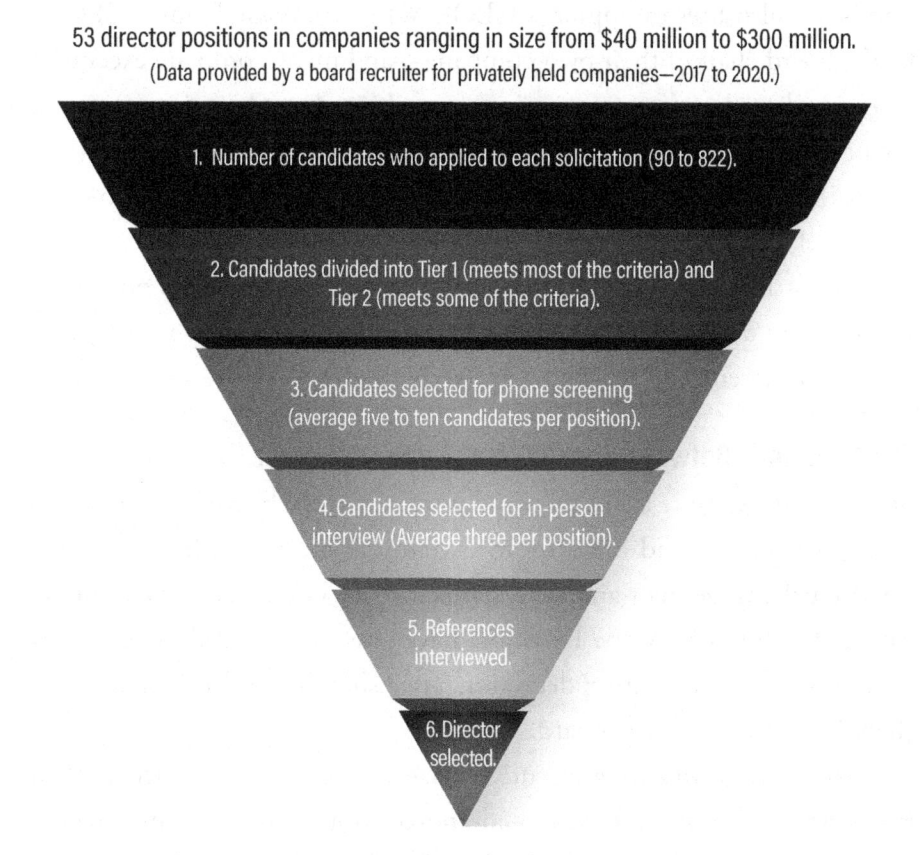

53 director positions in companies ranging in size from $40 million to $300 million.
(Data provided by a board recruiter for privately held companies—2017 to 2020.)

1. Number of candidates who applied to each solicitation (90 to 822).
2. Candidates divided into Tier 1 (meets most of the criteria) and Tier 2 (meets some of the criteria).
3. Candidates selected for phone screening (average five to ten candidates per position).
4. Candidates selected for in-person interview (Average three per position).
5. References interviewed.
6. Director selected.

C-Suite To Boardroom: The Traits An Experienced Executive Needs To Be An Effective Director

If you are an experienced CEO, CFO, or high-level executive, you may be thinking about putting your hat in the ring to be a board director of another company. Or perhaps you are the owner or a board member of a company looking for an outside, independent director. Either way, while it is true an experienced executive may make an effective board member, you must understand there are key differences between being a director and an executive.

Should a company's CEO also be on its board of directors? In the governance and management structure of a company, the CEO must consult the board of directors before making major, strategic moves for the company. The board also fires or appoints CEOs. While it's possible for a CEO to be the board chair of their own company—and many company executives sit on the board as directors to give internal insight—this raises questions about the monitoring of the company's direction. It also raises questions about the CEO's level of power, accountability, and the need for another high-level leader to raise important questions to the CEO.

This article focuses on appointing high-level executives as outside or independent directors for another company. Doing both jobs well requires two very different skill sets and leadership styles.

The Difference Between The CEO And A Board Director

Success in the C-suite is not the same as success in the boardroom. Director styles of behavior and boardroom dynamics require a collegial style of intellectual engagement and rigor. Directors are bound by both a duty of care and a duty of loyalty. Directors have grave responsibilities but they should not make operating decisions. They should not direct staff, other than direct reports to the board.

Candidates with strong executive styles tend to be very directive in their behaviors; they employ a command-and-control approach to interaction. Successful directors, on the other hand, need to be active listeners and highly collaborative. Demonstrating this style shift from the former to the latter is a critical part of the interview process, and candidates often fail to advance if they cannot quickly demonstrate their ability to behave as a good director should.

How To Demonstrate Your Suitability For A Board

Candidates need to be able to have a fierce argument in the boardroom and then enjoy a lunch break with the sparring partner.

Candidates also need to pass the airplane test. If current directors do not look forward to flying across the country sitting next to the candidate, why invite them to join as a board member?

As a board member candidate, here are a few things that should be watched during the interview process:

- Be mindful of your talk time. Listen more, talk less.
- Do not rush to fill dead airtime. Be patient and understand that silence is a sign of mental activity.
- Don't oversell yourself.
- Ask truly insightful questions that demonstrate your comprehension of the dialogue; don't just walk through a list of prepared questions.

Successful candidates need to demonstrate the judgment to properly balance the informational needs of everyone in the interview. It is a good test of how they will behave in the boardroom.

Candidates spend considerable effort to prepare their resume, bio, and cover letter; they have prepared their responses to the likely questions and studied the company and the industry. All that happens before walking into the first interview. You and all your competitors for the position have been granted the interview because you are all deemed to have the skills and experience to be a good director. The interviewers are likely focused on chemistry: does the candidate have the right temperament to fit the board and culture?

Candidates need to listen for verbal and non-verbal clues to adjust their behavior during the interview. Are you fitting in or not? Are you balancing leadership with the need to let other directors speak and lead when it is appropriate?

Understand The Executive And Directors' Roles

Experience as an executive is certainly a positive in terms of providing you with the skills and experience to be an effective director. You simply need to understand that the two jobs are indeed different, and they require very different styles.

Considering Public Company Executives For Private Boards

Private company owners sometimes get starry-eyed when they talk to public company executives who have run multibillion-dollar global enterprises. This is understandable since these people tend to be highly accomplished. They may be incredibly talented extroverts with engaging personalities. Attributes like these can be helpful to run a large public company. These executives can bring highly impactful experience and connections to a private company board.

While all of this is true, if you are considering adding this type of professional to your private company board, I suggest you evaluate them through a different lens.

Pay attention to scope. Private companies may have smaller, less developed management teams; less capital; and a narrower scope than their public counterparts. To be an effective director of a private company, a public company executive needs to adjust to the capabilities of the organization. This is a great example of what nominating chairs mean when they say, "We are concerned with fit."

Two stories capture this point succinctly. In a recent board meeting, I witnessed a director who was a senior executive from a Fortune 100 company say they wanted to bring in a consultant from a large, established organization, such as McKinsey, Bain, etc. While the directors agreed a consultant would be needed, I was surprised to hear those companies suggested. McKinsey and Bain focus on global corporations and national governments. The company under discussion made about $1 million each year in profits. It appeared the speaker did not consider the fit before making his recommendation.

In another situation, I observed a director from a $6 billion company who was explaining his company's HR philosophies; they were doing advanced work in certain areas. This was a useful education for the smaller business. However, it was clear an extraordinary effort would be needed to implement the suggestions. This director described the numerous VPs who were involved in pulling this program together. But the company in question had one VP who was known to be stretched thin.

In both cases, the speakers brought valuable information with good intent, but it was neither effective nor actionable due to the lack of fit between their experience and the realities of the organization in mind.

Evaluate for adaptability and the company culture. The culture, capabilities, and resources of a $50 billion global company are often very different from a $50 million private company. Large companies often have strong cultures with many unwritten but firm rules. If you do not comply, either the organization rejects you or you reject the organization. Smaller companies may not always be as formal, and their cultures can be more accepting since they need to be. Typically, everyone looks to how the owner behaves, and that is the culture.

In a large public company, sometimes the greatest competition comes from within the organization—leaders are vying for more authority and resources. In a smaller private company, there are often fewer games to be played since there are fewer players and less to fight over. Many things are simpler.

I have seen an inverse corollary when I have counseled public company executives who, for whatever reason, were looking for a new job. There are two observations I see time and again: First, if they do not get back onto the public company horse soon, e.g., within six to nine months, it is not likely to happen at all, and second, the rules in the private company world are very different. It can be more like a jungle, where you must figure things out at each turn. People who were successfully climbing the corporate ladder may lack the adaptability to succeed in the private company world.

This highlights how important the director selection process is for private companies. Even though public company candidates may have great experience and expertise, if they cannot couch their advice in an actionable manner for the business in question, it may have little value—and may even be a bit dangerous.

Find the right fit. After considering adaptability, personal style is an important point to evaluate. Oftentimes, a public company executive may be thought of as being a hard-charging, aggressive Type A personality. These characteristics can be critical to success in an operating position. But directors do not manage others; their role is to ask insightful questions, hold management accountable and focus on the strategy, oversight, capital structure, risk management, and management succession planning.

When considering a public company executive for a private company board, the candidate's ability to shift from delivering a P&L to knowing their role is "noses in, fingers out, and sensors on" is a critical point of evaluation.

These considerations are presented to inform the nominating committee to be thoughtful and diligent in screening candidates. If the public company executive can transition in a way that fits the needs of a smaller company, it could be a game changer. That person may have skills, experience, and relationships the smaller company would never have access to otherwise.

So when developing the candidate pool, think hard about the necessary criteria, and do not let the glamour of a large organization stop you from assessing how the candidate will fit in and perform in your boardroom.

Appendix C – **Acknowledgments**

I want to thank my publisher and editors at Indie Books International: Henry DeVries, Adrienne Moch, Devin DeVries, Lisa Lucas, Taylor Graham, Jazmin Barnes, and art director, Melissa Farr.

My first week working at Werner Co. included my first board meeting. During my tenure there, I learned many of the lessons that I have shared in this book. Unfortunately, it took another thirty years to realize what good schooling I had.

My dad was chair of the family business for over twenty years. I lead several boards now. As I prepare agendas, manage meetings, and wrestle with personalities, I am guided by the stories he would share at the dinner table.

Since then, I have seen the numerous variations in governance processes that exist in private companies. As with many things in life, I compared new experiences to my prior experiences to draw observations and conclusions. This comparative process highlighted that each governance system adapts to the needs of the organization and ownership group. But most owners can do better, if only with modest effort.

I wish to thank Dennis Kessler for his training, mentoring, and the generous use of his time and wisdom, much of which is implicitly and explicitly included herein. I would like to acknowledge the numerous fellow board members I have served with for the shared experiences and conversations that have helped me to develop my thoughts.

Thank you to my clients, referral sources, business partners, and investors for providing opportunities to impact the world.

But most of all, thank you to my family for supporting me in all my endeavors.

Appendix D – **About The Author**

Bruce Werner has served on private, family, VC, and PE portfolio company boards. His governance experience includes forming new boards and serving on established boards, both advisory and fiduciary, in addition to serving as a lead director. He has performed audit, governance, and compensation committee work.

In the non-profit world, Werner has served as board chair and worked on governance, nominating, strategy, compensation, finance, and investment committees.

Werner spent the first half of his career at Werner Ladder, with executive responsibilities in all facets of the business. During that time, the family completed six acquisitions and sustained 10 percent annual growth for over a decade. The family later exited the business in a successful LBO.

As an independent consultant, Werner helps owners address their governance, strategy, capital, talent, and succession issues. This work is based on several decades of deep operational experience. He has started and built businesses in finance, energy, retail, and technology, in addition to being a partner in a private equity fund.

Werner has a specialty of working with family businesses as an advisor and board member. An accomplished public speaker, he has connected with business audiences across the country on these same topics, working with Bank of America Private Bank, City National Bank, Vistage International, Families Enterprise & Wealth Conference, Cavendish Global Forum, Private Director Association, National Association of Home Builders, and the Turnaround Management Association. His academic relationships include

Northwestern's Kellogg School, Cornell's Smith Family Business Initiative, and Loyola University's Family Business Center.

Werner's first book, *Your Ownership Journey*, published in 2022, established his framework of ownership issues. In addition to numerous webinars and podcasts, he has been published in the *Private Company Director, Wealth Management, Estate Planning, Trusts & Estates*, and other national publications.

Werner received a BS in mechanical engineering/public policy from Carnegie-Mellon University. As an IBM Fellow, he graduated from Stanford University with an MS in manufacturing systems engineering. He completed his education at the MIT Sloan School, earning an MS management degree focusing on strategy and operations. To contact him, send an email to Bruce@KonaAdvisors.com.

Visit Bruce's website at
www.brucewerner.com

or view his profile at
www.linkedin.com/in/brucedwerner/.

Appendix E – **Works Referenced And Author's Notes**

[1] James Chen, "Corporate Governance Definition: How It Works, Principles, and Examples," Investopia, updated March 22,2023, investopedia.com/terms/c/corporategovernance.asp#:~:text= Governance percent20refers percent20specifically percent20to percent20the percent20set percent20of percent20rules percent2C,shareholders percent20are percent20important percent20stakeholders percent20who percent20can percent20affect percent20governance.

[2] "Why good corporate governance still matters in private companies," EY, June 28, 2019, https://www.ey.com/en_ae/assurance/why-good-corporate-governance-still-matters-in-private-companies.

[3] "1997 09 Statement on Corporate Governance", The Business Roundtable, September 1997, https://archive.org/details/6299567-1997-09-Statement-of-Corporate-Governance.

[4] Korn Ferry, "Advisory Boards: The Hot New Governance Trend," accessed May 9, 2023, https://www.kornferry.com/insights/briefings-for-the-boardroom/advisory-boards-new-governance-trends.

Advisory Board Centre, "State of the Market Global Report 2021," accessed May 9, 2023, https://www.advisoryboardcentre.com/our-research/state-of-the-market-global-report-2021/.

[5] Edwin Weathersby, "The 10 Greatest College Football Recruiting Head Coaches of All Time," February 17, 2011, https://bleacherreport.com/articles/612575-the-10-greatest-college-football-recruiting-head-coaches-of-all-time.

[6] "March Madness Gaming Estimates," American Gaming Association, accessed May 9, 2023, https://www.americangaming.org/resources/2023-march-madness-wagering-estimates/

[7] "Private Company Compensation and Governance Survey 2020 Summary Report," Private Company Director, accessed May 9, 2023, https://www.privatecompanydirector.com/landing-page/private-company-compensation-survey-2020.

[8] Brené Brown, *Daring Greatly: How the Courage to Be Vulnerable Transforms the Way We Live, Love, Parent, and Lead*, (New York: Avery Publishing, 2012).

[9] Michael Piellusch, "Is the chain of command still meaningful?," War Room, September 6, 2018, https://warroom.armywarcollege.edu/articles/chain-of-command/.

[10] Bruce D. Werner, "Getting Started: Private Company Compensation Committees," NACD Boardtalk, February 16, 2023,. https://blog.nacdonline.org/posts/start-private-compensation-committees.

[11] Pearl Zhu, *Digitizing Boardroom: The Multifaceted Aspects of Digital Ready Boards,* Lulu.com, April 23, 2018, https://www.lulu.com/shop/pearl-zhu/100-digital-pitfalls-how-to-overcome-pitfalls-on-the-path-of-going-digital/ebook/product-1q27qzg7.html?q=pearl+zhu&page=1&pageSize=4.

[12] Michael E. Porter, "How Competitive Forces Shape Strategy," *Harvard Business Review*, May 1979 (Vol. 57, No. 2).

[13] Alfred Chandler. *Strategy and Structure: Chapters in the History of the Industrial Enterprise*. (Cambridge: MIT Press,1962).

[14] Proverbs 24:6, The Bible.

[15] "Nationwide Survey Finds Majority of Business Owners Don't Have a Succession Plan," Nationwide.com, February 7, 2017, https://www.prnewswire.com/news-releases/nationwide-survey-finds-majority-of-business-owners-dont-have-a-succession-plan-300403316.html.

[16] Paul Hersey and Ken Blanchard derived this tool from the model of situational leadership they created in the 1970s.

[17] "Scout Motto," accessed May 10, 2023, https://www.boyscouttrail.com/boy-scouts/boy-scout-motto.asp.

[18] Spencer E. Ante, *Creative Capital: Georges Doriot and the Birth of Venture Capital*, (Cambridge: Harvard Business Review Press, 2008).

[19] "Understanding the Capital Stack and How It Affects Your Investments." JRW Investments, February 14, 2013, https://www.jrw.com/articles/investment-principles/understanding-the-capital-stack-and-how-it-affects-your-investments/.

[20] "What Are Black Swan Events? (Plus How to Identify One)," Indeed, June 24, 2022, https://www.indeed.com/career-advice/career-development/black-swan-events.

[21] Jay Campbell, "Encourage Your People to Give You Feedback," Blanchard LeaderChat, June 2, 2022, https://resources.kenblanchard.com/blanchard-leaderchat/encourage-your-people-to-give-you-feedback.

[22] "PNG Family Business Survey 2019," PWC, accessed May 10, 2023, https://www.pwc.com/pg/en/publications/family-business-survey/family-business-survey-2019.html.

[23] "QCA 2020 Non-Executive Directors Survey," NEDA, accessed May 10, 2023, https://www.nedaglobal.com/ned-insights/publications/qca-2020-non-executive-directors-survey/.

Appendix F – **Index**

Advisory boards, 21–23, 27, 36, 42, 44, 55, 62, 80, 86, 167, 169, 197
Audit committee, 17, 67, 74–76, 178

Benioff, Marc, 9
Blanchard, Ken, 151, 199
Blue Oak Strategy, vi, 101–102
Board action items, 67–69, 71
Board agenda, 64–72
Board candidates, 37–52, 177–192
Board charter, 25–27, 30, 36, 167
Board meeting minutes, 68
Bossidy, Lawrence, 53
Brown, Brené, 59, 198
Business Roundtable, 12, 24, 197
Bylaws, 14–15, 17, 27, 30, 36, 43, 91–92, 96, 160, 167, 172, 177

Carroll, Peter, 37–38
Chandler, Alfred, 99, 198
Compensation committee, vi, 67, 77, 79, 195, 198
Consulting boards, 22, 55, 62, 80, 169

D&O insurance, 43
Dementia, 157–160

Doriot, Georges, 131, 199
Ellison, Larry, 9
Financial Poise, vi
Junior advisory boards, 22, 80
Kessler, Dennis, iii, vi, 193
McClure, Tim, vi, 102
National Association of Corporate Directors (NACD), iv, vi, 31, 57, 112, 182, 185, 198
Nominating committee, 73, 80–81, 83, 171, 192

Ownership conflicts, 91–93

Porter, Michael, 97
Private Company Director Magazine, 56

Rohn, Jim, 97

Solman, Don, 9

The Badger Co, vi, 102–106

U.S. Army War College, 63

Zhu, Pearl, 85, 198

Appendix I - Index

Made in the USA
Monee, IL
21 November 2023